Introduction

Think of an analogy as a wonderful puzzle, and one has a great interdisciplinary teaching exercise.

An analogy is a type of comparison. An analogy is when a likeness is found between two unlike things. If approached as a puzzle, one solves the analogy by finding out how the pieces fit together. What links the words to each other? How can they be connected or tied together? What is the relationship between them?

> **cat** is to **meow** as **dog** is to ___**bark**___

Although the example above may appear to be easy, it is an exercise that involves cognitive processes and critical-thinking skills. One must comprehend the words read, categorize them, understand the connection between them, and then find a similar connection between a different pair of words. In this case, both *meow* and *bark* are sounds that a cat and dog make, respectively.

Analogies written for this series will focus on a variety of word relationships. They will develop, reinforce, and expand skills in the following areas:

→ visual imagery

→ reading comprehension

→ paying attention to detail (word sequence within word pairs)

→ vocabulary development

→ synonym, antonym, and homophone recognition and recall

→ understanding different shades of word meanings

→ reasoning

→ standardized-test taking

Students will be able to demonstrate mastery by doing the following:

→ working with both multiple-choice and write-out question formats

→ analyzing and fixing incorrect analogies

→ writing their own analogies in both question and sentence format

For interdisciplinary practice, some analogies will be subject-specific (addressing science, math, or social studies, for example). Others will push students to think outside of the box, as creative and imaginative connections between words will be asked for. Students may then explain in writing or verbally (depending on skill level) how they created analogous word pairs or situations.

Blank answer sheets can be found on page 60. Use these sheets to provide your students with practice in answering questions in a standardized-test format.

Introducing Analogies

Directions: Fill in the word you think should go in the blank.

1. **Sheep** is to **lamb** as **cow** is to _____.

2. **Sheep** is to **baa** as **cow** is to _____.

3. **Sheep** is to **wool** as **cow** is to _____.

4. **Sheep** is to **flock** as **cow** is to _____.

5. **Sheep** is to **ram** as **cow** is to _____.

What did you just do? You made an **analogy**! An analogy is a likeness in some ways between things that are otherwise unlike.

A lamb is not a calf, but a lamb is like a calf because they are both kinds of animal babies.

Sometimes analogies are written like this:

> **sheep : lamb :: cow : calf**

- The single colon (:) compares two items in a word pair.
- The double colon (::) compares the first word pair to the second word pair.

6. Rewrite question 2, 3, 4, or 5 in the analogy form using colons.

   _____ _____ _____ _____

Directions: Fill in the blanks to finish the analogies.

7. sister : brother :: female : _____

8. sister : brother :: aunt : _____

9. sister : brother :: mother : _____

10. sister : brother :: niece : _____

11. aunt : nephew :: uncle : _____

12. grandfather : grandmother :: _____ : _____

Editor
Eric Migliaccio

Editor in Chief
Ina Massler Levin, M.A.

Creative Director
Karen J. Goldfluss, M.S. Ed.

Illustrator
Renée Mc Elwee

Cover Artist
Brenda DiAntonis

Art Coordinator
Renée Mc Elwee

Imaging
Leonard P. Swierski

Publisher
Mary D. Smith, M.S. Ed.

Grade 5

TCR 3168

ANALOGIES
for
Critical Thinking

canoe : boat

truck : vehicle

A terrific way to:
- Sharpen logical thinking skills
- Prepare for standardized tests
- Understand word relationships
- Improve & develop vocabulary

Teacher Created Resources

Author
Ruth Foster, M.Ed.

Teacher Created Resources
12621 Western Avenue
Garden Grove, CA 92841
www.teachercreated.com
ISBN: 978-1-4206-3168-5

©2011 Teacher Created Resources
Reprinted, 2018
Made in U.S.A.

Teacher Created Resources

Table of Contents

Synonyms in Analogies

A **synonym** is a word that is nearly the **same** in meaning as another word.

1. Which word is not a synonym of the others?

   (A) decide　　　(B) conclude　　　(C) determine　　　(D) question

2. What answer makes the best analogy?

   (A) question : choose :: conclude : decide　　(C) determine : decide :: conclude : choose

   (B) conclude : determine :: question : decide　　(D) decide : conclude :: choose : question

Directions: Find the synonym that best completes the analogy.

3. **Leap** is to **bound** as **large** is to _____.

   (A) considerable　　(B) small　　　(C) jump　　　(D) laughable

4. **Late** is to **tardy** as **lately** is to _____.

   (A) hugely　　　(B) slowly　　　(C) dangerously　　(D) recently

5. **Positive** is to **sure** as **unlikely** is to _____.

   (A) beautiful　　(B) doubtful　　(C) peaceful　　(D) colorful

6. **Disagree** is to **argue** as **dig** is to _____.

   (A) excavate　　(B) explode　　(C) explore　　(D) explain

7. **Tie** is to **bind** as **bend** is to _____.

   (A) find　　　(B) flex　　　(C) straighten　　(D) strengthen

8. **Study** is to **examine** as **observe** is to _____.

   (A) steal　　　(B) explain　　(C) notice　　　(D) lose

Directions: Write down four answers. Only one answer should be correct!

9. **Fabulous** is to **fantastic** as **dangerous** is to _____.

   (A) _____　　(C) _____

   (B) _____　　(D) _____

10. Which one of your answers was correct? Write a sentence telling why. Use the word *synonym* in your sentence.

   _____

   _____

Antonyms in Analogies

An **antonym** is a word that is the **opposite** in meaning of another word.

1. Which word is an antonym of the others?

   Ⓐ ordinary　　　Ⓑ amazing　　　Ⓒ astonishing　　　Ⓓ marvelous

2. Which answer makes the best analogy?

   Ⓐ astonishing : marvelous :: amazing : ordinary　Ⓒ amazing : astonishing :: difficult : easy

   Ⓑ easy : difficult :: ordinary : marvelous　　　Ⓓ ordinary : astonishing :: marvelous : amazing

Directions: Find the antonym that best completes the analogy.

3. **Small** is to **enormous** as **serious** is to _____.

   Ⓐ sober　　　Ⓑ grim　　　Ⓒ witty　　　Ⓓ grave

4. **Shatter** is to **mend** as **break** is to _____.

   Ⓐ repair　　　Ⓑ shield　　　Ⓒ brilliant　　　Ⓓ rest

5. **Palace** is to **hut** as **shack** is to _____.

   Ⓐ shed　　　Ⓑ shanty　　　Ⓒ lean-to　　　Ⓓ castle

6. **Polite** is to **rude** as **respectful** is to _____.

   Ⓐ kind　　　Ⓑ impossible　　　Ⓒ impolite　　　Ⓓ sleepy

7. **Blunt** is to **sharp** as **curved** is to _____.

   Ⓐ broken　　　Ⓑ ball　　　Ⓒ round　　　Ⓓ straight

8. **Huge** is to **small** as **mammoth** is to _____.

   Ⓐ large　　　Ⓑ tiny　　　Ⓒ huge　　　Ⓓ gigantic

Directions: Write down four answers. Only one answer should be correct!

9. **Exit** is to **enter** as **start** is to _____.

   Ⓐ _____　　　Ⓒ _____

   Ⓑ _____　　　Ⓓ _____

10. Which one of your answers was correct? Write a sentence telling why. Use the word *antonym* in your sentence.

_____

_____

Synonym and Antonym Practice

Directions: Choose the answer that best completes the analogy. Write **synonyms** or **antonyms** on the blank line to describe how the question and answer words are related.

- Antonyms are words that are opposite in meaning.

- Synonyms are words that mean the same.

1. **fill : empty**
   - (A) limp : hobble
   - (B) lean : tilt
   - (C) let : allow
   - (D) loan : borrow

2. **rubbish : garbage**
   - (A) quarrel : fight
   - (B) child : adult
   - (C) part : all
   - (D) gather : spread

3. **welcome : greet**
   - (A) cheer : boo
   - (B) restrict : limit
   - (C) hit : pet
   - (D) finish : begin

4. **cooked : raw**
   - (A) mind : obey
   - (B) own : possess
   - (C) fact : fiction
   - (D) help : aid

5. **hero : champion**
   - (A) imposter : fake
   - (B) teacher : student
   - (C) doctor : patient
   - (D) baby : grownup

6. **plain : fancy**
   - (A) tight : loose
   - (B) shy : bashful
   - (C) wicked : evil
   - (D) silent : hushed

7. **clean : dirty**
   - (A) cut : snip
   - (B) hide : reveal
   - (C) shut : close
   - (D) eat : consume

8. **imitate : copy**
   - (A) edge : center
   - (B) create : ruin
   - (C) spend : save
   - (D) dwell : live

9. **weary : tired**
   - (A) elastic : rigid
   - (B) wealthy : poor
   - (C) honest : truthful
   - (D) sloppy : tidy

10. **hold : release**
    - (A) fold : crease
    - (B) stop : cease
    - (C) unite : divide
    - (D) smile : grin

11. **excite : bore**
    - (A) erupt : explode
    - (B) envy : desire
    - (C) equal : match
    - (D) tie : untie

12. **find : detect**
    - (A) shout : murmur
    - (B) whine : moan
    - (C) separate : mix
    - (D) end : commence

Synonym and Antonym Analogies

Directions: Write as many synonyms and antonyms as you can think of for the given words. Then, use a **thesaurus** to add even more words to your list.

	Synonyms	Antonyms
1. ooze		
2. optimistic		
3. terrible		
4. poor		
5. grow		

Directions: Write analogy questions using some of the words you wrote down. Two questions should be synonyms. Two questions should be antonyms.

6. _____ : _____

 Ⓐ _____ : _____

 Ⓑ _____ : _____

 Ⓒ _____ : _____

 Ⓓ _____ : _____

 Correct answer: _____ Synonym or antonym: _____

7. _____ : _____

 Ⓐ _____ : _____

 Ⓑ _____ : _____

 Ⓒ _____ : _____

 Ⓓ _____ : _____

 Correct answer: _____ Synonym or antonym: _____

8. _____ : _____

 Ⓐ _____ : _____

 Ⓑ _____ : _____

 Ⓒ _____ : _____

 Ⓓ _____ : _____

 Correct answer: _____ Synonym or antonym: _____

9. _____ : _____

 Ⓐ _____ : _____

 Ⓑ _____ : _____

 Ⓒ _____ : _____

 Ⓓ _____ : _____

 Correct answer: _____ Synonym or antonym: _____

Plurals

Directions: Think about how some words are singular (one) or plural (more than one). Then choose the answer that best completes each analogy. Pay attention to order!

| children : child | is not the same as | child : children |

---

1. **children : child** is

   Ⓐ singular : plural

   Ⓑ plural : singular

2. **child : children** is

   Ⓐ singular : plural

   Ⓑ plural : singular

---

3. **house : houses**

   Ⓐ mouse : mouses

   Ⓑ mouse : mice

   Ⓒ mouses : mouse

   Ⓓ mice : mouse

4. **men : man**

   Ⓐ dice : die

   Ⓑ person : people

   Ⓒ woman : women

   Ⓓ ox : oxen

5. **tooth : teeth**

   Ⓐ mouths : mouth

   Ⓑ feet : foot

   Ⓒ toes : toe

   Ⓓ finger : fingers

---

6. **half : halves**

   Ⓐ loaf : loafs

   Ⓑ loaf : loafes

   Ⓒ loaf : loaves

   Ⓓ loaf : loavess

7. **tomatoes : tomato**

   Ⓐ volcanoes : volcanoe

   Ⓑ volcanoe : volcanoes

   Ⓒ potatoes : potato

   Ⓓ potato : potatoes

8. **wife : wives**

   Ⓐ knives : knife

   Ⓑ knives : knive

   Ⓒ life : lifes

   Ⓓ life : lives

---

9. **nucleus : nuclei**

   Ⓐ cactus : cacti

   Ⓑ desserts : desert

   Ⓒ sands : sand

   Ⓓ fungi : fungus

10. **geese : goose**

   Ⓐ swan : swans

   Ⓑ deer : deer

   Ⓒ glass : glasses

   Ⓓ plate : plates

11. **pants : pants**

   Ⓐ duck : duckling

   Ⓑ roosters : hens

   Ⓒ horse : cattle

   Ⓓ sheep : sheep

---

12. Write your own analogy using singular and plural words. Make sure only one of your answers is correct!

    _____ : _____

    Ⓐ_____ : _____   Ⓒ_____ : _____

    Ⓑ_____ : _____   Ⓓ_____ : _____

Adjectives

Adjectives are often used in analogies. An adjective is a word that describes a noun. Adjectives answer three questions:

1. What kind is it?   *2.* How many are there?   *3.* Which one is it?

Directions: Fill in the blanks and find the answer that best completes the analogies.

1. In the word pair [**bright : sun**], the word ___b_____· _____ is an
   ___a_____ because it tells what kind of sun it is.

2. In the word pair [**ringed : planet**], the word _____ is an
   _____ because it tells what kind of planet it is.

3. **dancer : graceful**	*4.* **map : flat**	*5.* **tropics : sweltering**
Ⓐ telephone : talk	Ⓐ globe : round	Ⓐ freezing : Arctic
Ⓑ talk : telephone	Ⓑ legend : key	Ⓑ elephant : ears
Ⓒ flexible : gymnast	Ⓒ compass : west	Ⓒ leopard : spotted
Ⓓ gymnast : flexible	Ⓓ ocean : land	Ⓓ striped : tiger
6. **flower : fragrant**	*7.* **hook : barbed**	*8.* **crackers : crunchy**
Ⓐ ball : round	Ⓐ dark : cave	Ⓐ nurse : hospital
Ⓑ stove : kitchen	Ⓑ mesa : flat	Ⓑ pilot : helicopter
Ⓒ brick : chimney	Ⓒ green : pea	Ⓒ corn : maize
Ⓓ enormous : castle	Ⓓ funny : clown	Ⓓ mayor : elected
9. **brief : second**	*10.* **tart : lime**	*11.* **cotton : cloth**
Ⓐ decade : ten	Ⓐ fire : hot	Ⓐ aluminum : can
Ⓑ minute : sixty	Ⓑ pickle : sour	Ⓑ table : wood
Ⓒ long : century	Ⓒ rabbit : foot	Ⓒ bottle : plastic
Ⓓ year : month	Ⓓ sharp : tack	Ⓓ ball : rubber

12. Think of three adjectives that might be used to describe each noun.

   • ocean   _____   _____   _____

   • pond   _____   _____   _____

13. Make an analogy using words and answers from Question 12.

   _____ : _____ :: _____ : _____

What People Use

Some word pairs in analogies are connected by what people use or need in their jobs.

Examples: painter : brush (*person* to *what he/she uses*)

brush : painter (*what he/she uses* to *person*)

Directions: Choose the answer that best completes each analogy. Then write down other items the person in the question might use.

---

1. **carpenter : saw**

(A) pencil : paper

(B) paper : pencil

(C) sword : knight

(D) knight : sword

ruler, _____

2. **hose : firefighter**

(A) gardener : hoe

(B) chisel : sculptor

(C) writer : pen

(D) baker : oven

_____

3. **pilot : plane**

(A) captain : ship

(B) paddle : canoe

(C) teacher : student

(D) truck : driver

_____

---

4. **spoon : cook**

(A) bowl : stir

(B) astronaut : star

(C) map : navigator

(D) weaver : loom

_____

5. **plumber : wrench**

(A) axe : logger

(B) computer : screen

(C) doctor : patient

(D) builder : crane

_____

6. **swimmer : goggles**

(A) horse : jockey

(B) archer : bow

(C) ball : kick

(D) player : fan

_____

---

7. **tractor : farmer**

(A) fisherman : boat

(B) general : army

(C) train : engineer

(D) desk : classroom

_____

8. **tailor : scissors**

(A) waiter : tray

(B) pick : miner

(C) writer : read

(D) rope : climber

_____

9. **scrubs : surgeon**

(A) cook : apron

(B) detective : clue

(C) costume : actor

(D) bloodhound : scent

_____

---

10. Write three analogies using some of the items you wrote down.

_____ : _____ :: _____ : _____

_____ : _____ :: _____ : _____

_____ : _____ :: _____ : _____

Things that Go Together

Directions: Write down what you think of when you read these words:

(There are no wrong answers. Just write down the first thing you think of.)

1. do's and _____

2. black and _____

3. bread and _____

4. table and _____

5. pencil and _____

Check to see if the person sitting next to you or other students in your class thought of the same things.

Directions: Choose the answer that best completes each analogy. The connection between the word pairs is *things or words that go together.* (**Hint:** Say the underlined words with the word *and* between them; for example, "cold *and* grey.")

1. **Cold** is to **grey** as **fast** is to _____.
   - Ⓐ furious
   - Ⓑ fat
   - Ⓒ family
   - Ⓓ friend

2. **Life** is to **times** as **odds** is to _____.
   - Ⓐ flowers
   - Ⓑ paints
   - Ⓒ ends
   - Ⓓ trains

3. **Salt** is to **pepper** as **sugar** is to _____.
   - Ⓐ white
   - Ⓑ spice
   - Ⓒ drink
   - Ⓓ fruit

4. **Peas** is to **carrots** as **apples** is to _____.
   - Ⓐ tomatoes
   - Ⓑ oranges
   - Ⓒ corn
   - Ⓓ grapefruit

5. **Tried** is to **true** as **leaps** is to _____.
   - Ⓐ bunny
   - Ⓑ sleep
   - Ⓒ horses
   - Ⓓ bounds

6. **Cup** is to **saucer** as **shoes** is to _____.
   - Ⓐ leather
   - Ⓑ toes
   - Ⓒ plate
   - Ⓓ socks

7. **Now** is to **then** as **give** is to _____.
   - Ⓐ seek
   - Ⓑ help
   - Ⓒ take
   - Ⓓ donate

8. **Peace** is to **quiet** as **safe** is to _____.
   - Ⓐ sound
   - Ⓑ awake
   - Ⓒ total
   - Ⓓ seatbelt

Past and Present

A **verb** is an **action** word. A verb tells you what you are doing. Verbs have different tenses: the **present** tense is for an action that is happening now, and the **past** tense is for an action that has already happened.

Directions: Look at the chart below. Write down two more examples using different verbs.

Present		Past	
Today I	catch	*Yesterday I*	slept
Today I	jump	*Yesterday I*	ate
Today I		*Yesterday I*	
Today I		*Yesterday I*	

Directions: Choose a word from the word box that best completes each analogy. (Be careful! Some of the words in the word box are not proper words.)

bring	go	plea	leaved	find
bringed	goed	pled	left	finded
brought	went	pleat	leave	found
push	speak	rode	hurt	quit
pushed	speaked	ride	hurted	quitted
pusht	spought	rided	hurtted	quits

1. bite : bit :: bring : _____

2. kick : kicked :: push : _____

3. ran : run :: went : _____

4. slept : sleep :: spoke : _____

5. beg : begged :: plead : _____

6. rose : rise :: rode : _____

7. wrote : write :: left : _____

8. set : set :: hurt : _____

9. wear : wore :: find : _____

10. upset : upset :: quit : _____

11. Write down the question numbers of the ones that were

   • present to past: _____   • synonyms: _____

   • past to present: _____   • impossible to tell: _____

Past and Present 2

Directions: These analogies are based on past and present verb tenses. Something **past** has already happened. Something **present** is now. Choose the answer that best completes each analogy. Pay attention to order, and watch out for spelling errors! (For example, *meaned* is not a word. The past tense of *mean* is *meant*.)

1. **fly : flew**

   Ⓐ present : past

   Ⓑ past : present

2. **flew : fly**

   Ⓐ present : past

   Ⓑ past : present

3. **sing : sang :: catch :**

   Ⓐ catching   Ⓒ catches

   Ⓑ catched   Ⓓ caught

4. **called : call :: grew :**

   Ⓐ grown   Ⓒ grow

   Ⓑ growed   Ⓓ growing

5. **look : looked**

   Ⓐ speak : spoke   Ⓒ speak : speaked

   Ⓑ spoke : speak   Ⓓ speaked : speak

6. **built : build**

   Ⓐ fought : fight   Ⓒ eated : eat

   Ⓑ fight : fought   Ⓓ eat : eated

7. **shut : shut**

   Ⓐ drawed : drawed   Ⓒ cut : cut

   Ⓑ weeped : weeped   Ⓓ keept : keept

8. **wind : wound**

   Ⓐ mixed : mix   Ⓒ fixt : fix

   Ⓑ mix : mixed   Ⓓ fix : fixt

9. **skied : ski**

   Ⓐ saw : seen   Ⓒ see : saw

   Ⓑ seen : saw   Ⓓ saw : see

10. **hurry : hurried**

    Ⓐ bringed : bring   Ⓒ brought : bring

    Ⓑ bring : bringed   Ⓓ bring : brought

11. Write down the past and present tense of two verbs. The verbs you list should not be in the questions.

	Present	Past
1.		
2.		

12. Make an analogy using your verbs from Question 11.

_____ : _____ :: _____ : _____

Purpose

Some analogies are based on how things can be used, or what their purposes are.

Directions: Choose the answer that best completes each analogy. Pay attention to order! (For example, | **dam : block** | is not the same as | **block : dam** |.)

1. **dam : block** is
   - (A) thing : purpose
   - (B) purpose : thing

2. **block : dam** is
   - (A) thing : purpose
   - (B) purpose : thing

3. **scale : weigh :: thermometer :**
   - (A) location
   - (C) temperature
   - (B) humidity
   - (D) time

4. **scope : spot :: alarm :**
   - (A) ring
   - (C) clock
   - (B) warn
   - (D) buzz

5. **nose : smell**
   - (A) skin : burn
   - (C) taste : tongue
   - (B) hear : ear
   - (D) eye : observe

6. **scissors : cut**
   - (A) cool : refrigerator
   - (C) sandal : toe
   - (B) iron : wrinkle
   - (D) ruler : measure

7. **draw : pencil**
   - (A) ink : black
   - (C) color : crayon
   - (B) fold : paper
   - (D) erase : mark

8. **kite : fly**
   - (A) arrow : shoot
   - (C) catch : fish
   - (B) kick : ball
   - (D) chew : food

9. **broom : sweep**
   - (A) sip : straw
   - (C) shovel : scoop
   - (B) sleep : bed
   - (D) sit : chair

10. **pedal : bike**
    - (A) trampoline : jump
    - (C) tiger : train
    - (B) type : computer
    - (D) towel : dry

Directions: Fill in the blanks to make your own analogies. The connection between the word pairs should be | **thing : use/purpose** | or | **use/purpose : thing** |.

11. _____television_____ : _____ :: _____ : _____

12. _____sew_____ : _____ :: _____ : _____

Where Things Go

Some analogies are based on where things go, live, or are found.

Directions: Choose the answer that best completes each analogy.

Pay attention to order: | **picture : wall** | is not the same as | **wall : picture** |.

1. **picture : wall**
   - Ⓐ thing : where goes
   - Ⓑ where goes : thing

2. **wall : picture**
   - Ⓐ thing : where goes
   - Ⓑ where goes : thing

3. **carpet : floor**
   - Ⓐ fan : ceiling
   - Ⓒ ceiling : white
   - Ⓑ floor : ceiling
   - Ⓓ ceiling : rug

4. **squirrel : tree**
   - Ⓐ stream : trout
   - Ⓒ pond : frog
   - Ⓑ octopus : ocean
   - Ⓓ desert : tiger

5. **stairs : house**
   - Ⓐ parachute : jump
   - Ⓒ climb : rise
   - Ⓑ kitchen : hall
   - Ⓓ elevator : skyscraper

6. **pot : stove**
   - Ⓐ toaster : toast
   - Ⓒ blender : mix
   - Ⓑ computer : desk
   - Ⓓ kitchen : oven

7. **car : garage**
   - Ⓐ station : train
   - Ⓒ plane : hangar
   - Ⓑ dock : boat
   - Ⓓ closet : coat

8. **desert : cactus**
   - Ⓐ marsh : reed
   - Ⓒ prairie : bear
   - Ⓑ fern : forest
   - Ⓓ seaweed : ocean

9. **scarf : neck**
   - Ⓐ finger : ring
   - Ⓒ belt : buckle
   - Ⓑ finger : knuckle
   - Ⓓ belt : waist

10. **lobster : ocean**
    - Ⓐ antelope : sea
    - Ⓒ bison : prairie
    - Ⓑ lion : swamp
    - Ⓓ octopus : forest

11. Think of two animals to complete the analogy correctly.

    _____ : _____tropics_____ :: _____ : _____tundra_____

12. Think of two items to complete the analogy correctly.

    _____firetruck_____ : _____ :: _____ambulance_____ : _____

Animal Family Names

Some analogies are based on the names of *old*, *young*, *male* and *female* family members.

Directions: Choose the answer that best completes each analogy.

Pay attention to order: | **cat : kitten** | is not the same as | **kitten : cat** |.

1. **alligator : hatchling** is
   - Ⓐ old : young
   - Ⓑ young : old

2. **hatchling : alligator** is
   - Ⓐ old : young
   - Ⓑ young : old

3. **colt : boy :: filly :**
   - Ⓐ foal
   - Ⓒ stallion
   - Ⓑ girl
   - Ⓓ mare

4. **drake : duck :: stallion :**
   - Ⓐ lion
   - Ⓒ horse
   - Ⓑ fox
   - Ⓓ duckling

5. **doe : fawn**
   - Ⓐ ewe : lamb
   - Ⓒ chick : dog
   - Ⓑ pig : sheep
   - Ⓓ rooster : chicken

6. **elephant : bull**
   - Ⓐ seal : pup
   - Ⓒ pig : boar
   - Ⓑ whale : cow
   - Ⓓ goat : kid

7. **mare : horse**
   - Ⓐ rooster : hen
   - Ⓒ goose : gander
   - Ⓑ cub : lion
   - Ⓓ vixen : fox

8. **butterfly : larva**
   - Ⓐ maggot : fly
   - Ⓒ male : female
   - Ⓑ frog : tadpole
   - Ⓓ young : old

9. **calf : cow**
   - Ⓐ puppy : dog
   - Ⓒ duck : gosling
   - Ⓑ cat : kitten
   - Ⓓ tiger : cub

10. **turkey : tom**
    - Ⓐ bull : moose
    - Ⓒ calf : yak
    - Ⓑ chick : ostrich
    - Ⓓ zebra : stallion

Directions: Use animal names to complete the analogies correctly. Here are some hints:
- Invertebrates are animals without a backbone or spinal column.
- Vertebrates are animals with a backbone or spinal column.

11. <u>invertebrate</u> : <u>vertebrate</u> :: _____ : _____

12. _____ : <u>vertebrate</u> :: _____ : <u>invertebrate</u>

Finding the Connection

Directions: Answer the analogies. Then write down the connection between the word pairs.

1. bird : feather
- Ⓐ dog : pup
- Ⓑ dog : tail
- Ⓒ dog : fur
- Ⓓ dog : bark

2. turtle : shell
- Ⓐ fur : otter
- Ⓑ feather : eagle
- Ⓒ scale : snake
- Ⓓ armadillo : plate

3. orange : peel
- Ⓐ apple : skin
- Ⓑ rind : melon
- Ⓒ shell : peanut
- Ⓓ bark : tree

4. What is the connection in #1–3? _____

Now write two of your own word pairs that have the same connection. If needed, you may mix up words from the questions and answer choices to make your own analogies.

5. _____ : _____ **6.** _____ : _____

7. jam : jar
- Ⓐ milk : white
- Ⓑ milk : carton
- Ⓒ milk : cow
- Ⓓ milk : cheese

8. feather : pillow
- Ⓐ flowerpot : dirt
- Ⓑ sandbag : sand
- Ⓒ classroom : desk
- Ⓓ letter : envelope

9. air : balloon
- Ⓐ water : splash
- Ⓑ water : drink
- Ⓒ water : canteen
- Ⓓ water : boil

10. What is the connection in #7–9? _____

Now write two of your own word pairs that have the same connection. If needed, you may mix up words from the questions and answer choices to make your own analogies.

11. _____ : _____ **12.** _____ : _____

13. vein : blood
- Ⓐ canal : water
- Ⓑ oil : pipeline
- Ⓒ attic : house
- Ⓓ sound : air

14. vase : flowers
- Ⓐ books : shelf
- Ⓑ closet : clothes
- Ⓒ picture : frame
- Ⓓ drawer : desk

15. bowl : soup
- Ⓐ spoon : fork
- Ⓑ plate : cup
- Ⓒ glass : juice
- Ⓓ butter : knife

16. What is the connection in #13–15? _____

Now write two of your own word pairs that have the same connection. If needed, you may mix up words from the questions and answer choices to make your own analogies.

17. _____ : _____ **18.** _____ : _____

Finding the Connection 2

Directions: Answer the analogies. Then write down the connection between the word pairs.

1. **fang : snake**

Ⓐ mane : lion

Ⓑ fin : dolphin

Ⓒ whisker : cat

Ⓓ tusk : elephant

2. **gills : fish**

Ⓐ lungs : cat

Ⓑ paws : dog

Ⓒ stripes : skunk

Ⓓ spots : leopard

3. **claw : bear**

Ⓐ feather : eagle

Ⓑ talon : eagle

Ⓒ hunt : eagle

Ⓓ tooth : eagle

4. What is the connection in #1–3? _____

Now write an analogy of your own with the same connection. If needed, you may mix up words from the questions and answer choices to make your own analogies.

5. _____ : _____ :: _____ : _____

6. **octopus : arm**

Ⓐ arm : starfish

Ⓑ leg : boy

Ⓒ squid : tentacle

Ⓓ neck : giraffe

7. **whale : flipper**

Ⓐ monkey : arm

Ⓑ wing : bird

Ⓒ claw : tiger

Ⓓ scale : snake

8. **elephant : trunk**

Ⓐ muzzle : dog

Ⓑ beak : falcon

Ⓒ face : panther

Ⓓ pig : snout

9. What is the connection in #6–8? _____

How is the order in this connection different from question 4? _____

Now write an analogy of your own with the same connection. If needed, you may mix up words from the questions and answer choices to make your own analogies.

10. _____ : _____ :: _____ : _____

11. **god : goddess**

Ⓐ actress : actor

Ⓑ actor : actress

Ⓒ master : servant

Ⓓ servant : master

12. **duke : duchess**

Ⓐ queen : king

Ⓑ prince : princess

Ⓒ duchess : duke

Ⓓ lady : knight

13. **waiter : waitress**

Ⓐ mother : father

Ⓑ niece : aunt

Ⓒ uncle : nephew

Ⓓ host : hostess

14. What is the connection in #11–13? _____

Now write an analogy of your own with the same connection. If needed, you may mix up words from the questions and answer choices to make your own analogies.

15. _____ : _____ :: _____ : _____

Finding the Connection 3

Directions: Answer the analogies. Then write down the connection between the word pairs.

1. **stage : actor**
- Ⓐ kitchen : cook
- Ⓑ pilot : plane
- Ⓒ farmer : field
- Ⓓ movie : screen

2. **lab : scientist**
- Ⓐ doctor : hospital
- Ⓑ classroom : teacher
- Ⓒ book : library
- Ⓓ clerk : store

3. **office : secretary**
- Ⓐ runner : track
- Ⓑ student : school
- Ⓒ court : judge
- Ⓓ artist : studio

4. What is the connection in #1–3? _____

Now write an analogy of your own with the same connection. If needed, you may mix up words from the questions and answer choices to make your own analogies.

5. _____ : _____ :: _____ : _____

6. **snake : slither**
- Ⓐ hop : rabbit
- Ⓑ build : beaver
- Ⓒ skunk : stripe
- Ⓓ worm : wiggle

7. **monkey : swing**
- Ⓐ swim : fish
- Ⓑ kangaroo : jump
- Ⓒ penguin : fly
- Ⓓ deer : dig

8. **eagle : soar**
- Ⓐ jellyfish : float
- Ⓑ shark : fly
- Ⓒ run : cheetah
- Ⓓ climb : lizard

9. What is the connection in #6–8? _____

Now write an analogy of your own with the same connection. If needed, you may mix up words from the questions and answer choices to make your own analogies.

10. _____ : _____ :: _____ : _____

11. **sticker : car**
- Ⓐ ant : march
- Ⓑ cat : fur
- Ⓒ shoe : clown
- Ⓓ tick : dog

12. **barnacle : ship**
- Ⓐ stamp : colorful
- Ⓑ stamp : letter
- Ⓒ stamp : envelope
- Ⓓ stamp : address

13. **magnet : iron**
- Ⓐ paste : water
- Ⓑ tape : clear
- Ⓒ honey : eat
- Ⓓ glue : paper

14. What is the connection in #11–13? _____

Now write an analogy of your own with the same connection. If needed, you may mix up words from the questions and answer choices to make your own analogies.

15. _____ : _____ :: _____ : _____

Trying Out the Connection

Directions: Write out how the word pairs are connected.

1. **hill : mountain**

• A h_____ is less than or smaller than a m_____.

2. **employ : hire**

• If you e_____ something, you h_____ it.

3. **triangle : shape**

• A t_____ is a kind of s_____.

Directions: Fill in the words to see what word pair is the correct answer (it will be the only one that makes sense). Then circle the correct answer.

4. **hill : mountain**

Ⓐ fish : water   Ⓑ lake : puddle   Ⓒ reservoir : dam   Ⓓ brook : river

• A f_____ is less than or smaller than a w_____.

• A l_____ is less than or smaller than a p_____.

• A r_____ is less than or smaller than a d_____.

• A b_____ is less than or smaller than a r_____.

5. **employ : hire**

Ⓐ correct : err   Ⓑ erase : write   Ⓒ proofread : check   Ⓓ pencil : tablet

• If you c_____ something, you e_____ it.

• If you e_____ something, you w_____ it.

• If you p_____ something, you c_____ it.

• If you p_____ something, you t_____ it.

6. **triangle : shape**

Ⓐ cardinal : bird   Ⓑ falcon : hunt   Ⓒ feather : sparrow   Ⓓ dove : parrot

• A c_____ is a kind of b_____.

• A f_____ is a kind of h_____.

• A f_____ is a kind of s_____.

• A d_____ is a kind of p_____.

Part to Whole

Some word pairs in analogies are connected by *part to whole* or *whole to part*.

- **Examples:** day : week (*part to whole*)

  week : day (*whole to part*)

Directions: Choose the answer that best completes each analogy and answer the questions.

1. **student : class** Ⓐ conductor : flute Ⓑ flute : conductor Ⓒ orchestra : musician Ⓓ musician : orchestra	*2.* **cage : bars** Ⓐ jail : prison Ⓑ fence : stakes Ⓒ pen : trap Ⓓ strand : rope	*3.* **lead : pencil** Ⓐ crayon : wax Ⓑ marker : color Ⓒ ink : pen Ⓓ eraser : mistake
4. **screen : television** Ⓐ monitor : computer Ⓑ mouse : pad Ⓒ keyboard : type Ⓓ printer : paper	*5.* **train : boxcar** Ⓐ car : drive Ⓑ ship : canoe Ⓒ petal : flower Ⓓ forest : tree	*6.* **tooth : comb** Ⓐ bristle : brush Ⓑ button : push Ⓒ cake : slice Ⓓ book : page
7. **constellation : star** Ⓐ Earth : planet Ⓑ tail : comet Ⓒ solar system : sun Ⓓ moon : distant	*8.* **sentence : word** Ⓐ sing : voice Ⓑ scale : note Ⓒ stick : drum Ⓓ song : write	*9.* **cushion : couch** Ⓐ table : cloth Ⓑ chair : pad Ⓒ mattress : bed Ⓓ floor : rug
10. **dresser : drawer** Ⓐ bookcase : shelf Ⓑ brick : chimney Ⓒ step : staircase Ⓓ clothes : closet	*11.* **necklace : bead** Ⓐ finger : toe Ⓑ bracelet : arm Ⓒ floor : building Ⓓ house : room	*12.* **chapter : book** Ⓐ month : week Ⓑ act : play Ⓒ garden : weeds Ⓓ season : fall

13. List the questions that were

- part to whole: ___1,_____   • whole to part: _____

14. Write your own analogy using four of these words: **kernel, pumpkin, lettuce, corn, leaf, carrot.**

_____ : _____ :: _____ : _____

Is your analogy *part to whole* or *whole to part*? _____

Less Than/More Than

Some analogies are based on less than/more than. One word in the word pair might be smaller than, bigger than, or not as strong or intense as the other word.

Directions: Choose the answer that best completes each analogy. (Remember to pay attention to order: | **breathe : pant** | is not the same as | **pant : breathe** |.)

1. **pant : breathe** is
   - Ⓐ less than : more than
   - Ⓑ more than : less than

2. **breathe : pant** is
   - Ⓐ less than : more than
   - Ⓑ more than : less than

3. **thirsty : parched**
   - Ⓐ battle : argue
   - Ⓑ argue : battle
   - Ⓒ float : sink
   - Ⓓ sink : float

4. **ask : plead**
   - Ⓐ enter : exit
   - Ⓑ exit : enter
   - Ⓒ flee : leave
   - Ⓓ leave : flee

5. **dampen : drench**
   - Ⓐ tire : exhaust
   - Ⓑ stare : glance
   - Ⓒ water : hose
   - Ⓓ spray : sprinkle

6. **starved : hungry**
   - Ⓐ okay : fantastic
   - Ⓑ pretty : gorgeous
   - Ⓒ big : enormous
   - Ⓓ magnificent : good

7. **order : tell**
   - Ⓐ phone : talk
   - Ⓑ stroll : race
   - Ⓒ toss : hurl
   - Ⓓ love : like

8. **call : scream**
   - Ⓐ guzzle : sip
   - Ⓑ bite : nip
   - Ⓒ cry : sob
   - Ⓓ boil : warm

9. **snack : feast**
   - Ⓐ mischievous : evil
   - Ⓑ shout : whisper
   - Ⓒ roar : giggle
   - Ⓓ bang : tap

10. **wipe : scrub**
    - Ⓐ touch : press
    - Ⓑ drive : car
    - Ⓒ dark : dim
    - Ⓓ leap : frog

11. **destroy : harm**
    - Ⓐ read : study
    - Ⓑ chirp : screech
    - Ⓒ hit : pound
    - Ⓓ gush : drip

12. Use four of these phrases to make an analogy: **"say you will," "look at," "fond of," "swear to," "devoted to."**

    _____ : _____ :: _____ : _____

13. Make your own analogy with a less than/more than relationship. You may use single words or phrases.

    _____ : _____ :: _____ : _____

Classifying Analogies

Some analogies are based on how things can be grouped, or how they can be classified.

Directions: Fill in the blanks and choose the answer that best completes each analogy.

1. How are robins and parrots alike?

   • They are both kinds of _b_____.

2. How are sneakers and boots alike?

   • They are both kinds of _s_____.

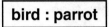

Pay attention to order: | **parrot : bird** | is not the same as | **bird : parrot** |.

A *parrot* is always a *bird*. A *bird* is not always a *parrot*.

---

3. **parrot** is to **bird** as

   Ⓐ shoe : boot

   Ⓑ boot : shoe

4. **flower** is to **daisy** as

   Ⓐ furniture : couch

   Ⓑ couch : furniture

5. **mammal** is to **hippopotamus**

   Ⓐ triceratops : dinosaur

   Ⓑ dinosaur : triceratops

6. **iron** is to **metal** as

   Ⓐ pepper : spice

   Ⓑ spice : pepper

7. **stove** is to **appliance** as

   Ⓐ grain : wheat

   Ⓑ wheat : grain

8. **vegetable** is to **carrot** as

   Ⓐ watermelon : fruit

   Ⓑ fruit : watermelon

9. **quartz** is to **mineral** as

   Ⓐ sedimentary : rock

   Ⓑ rock : sedimentary

10. **rodent** is to **mouse** as

    Ⓐ frog : amphibian

    Ⓑ amphibian : frog

11. **knee** is to **joint** as

    Ⓐ shirt : clothing

    Ⓑ clothing : shirt

12. **computer** is to **laptop** as

    Ⓐ beverage : milk

    Ⓑ milk : beverage

Classifying Analogies 2

Directions: Fill in the blanks and choose the answer that best completes each analogy.

1. How are a screwdriver and a hammer alike?

   • They are both t _____.

2. How are these pairs different? | screwdriver : tool | | tool : screwdriver |

   • A s _____ is always a _____.

   • A t _____ is not always a _____.

---

3. **greyhound : dog**
   - Ⓐ oak : tree
   - Ⓑ tree : oak
   - Ⓒ pine : elm
   - Ⓓ elm : pine

4. **truck : vehicle**
   - Ⓐ boat : canoe
   - Ⓑ canoe : boat
   - Ⓒ raft : paddle
   - Ⓓ paddle : raft

5. **hip hop : music**
   - Ⓐ beat : drum
   - Ⓑ strum : guitar
   - Ⓒ socks : shoes
   - Ⓓ skirt : clothes

6. **cello : instrument**
   - Ⓐ color : green
   - Ⓑ fruit : strawberry
   - Ⓒ spoon : utensil
   - Ⓓ table : chair

7. **bird : vulture**
   - Ⓐ tea : drink
   - Ⓑ python : snake
   - Ⓒ flower : violet
   - Ⓓ hearing : sense

8. **leopard : cat**
   - Ⓐ tiger : cheetah
   - Ⓑ salmon : fish
   - Ⓒ rodent : rat
   - Ⓓ game : baseball

9. **Canada : country**
   - Ⓐ Ohio : state
   - Ⓑ city : New York
   - Ⓒ lake : Superior
   - Ⓓ mountain : Everest

10. **novel : book**
    - Ⓐ dog : poodle
    - Ⓑ desk : chair
    - Ⓒ dessert : pie
    - Ⓓ diamond : gem

11. **cinnamon : spice**
    - Ⓐ alligator : reptile
    - Ⓑ mammal : dolphin
    - Ⓒ insect : cricket
    - Ⓓ vegetable : spinach

---

12. Create two answer choices for this word pair: | month : January | . Make sure only one answer choice is correct.

    Ⓐ _____ : planet   Ⓑ planet : _____

13. Tell which answer for question 12 is correct and why. _____

_____

Practice Making Classes

Directions: Think of the names of as many things as you can that fit in the given classes.

Class	Class Members or Items
1. carnivores *(consume meat)*	
2. herbivores *(consume plants)*	
3. omnivores *(consume plants and animals)*	
4. aquatic *(living in or on water)*	
5. arboreal *(living in trees)*	
6. subterranean *(underground)*	

Directions: Write two analogy questions using class names and some of the things you listed as members of each class. One question should have the class first, then an item. One question should have an item first and then the class.

7. _____ : _____

Ⓐ _____ : _____

Ⓑ _____ : _____

Ⓒ _____ : _____

Ⓓ _____ : _____

Correct answer: _____

Is your answer *class to member* or *member to class*? _____

8. _____ : _____

Ⓐ _____ : _____

Ⓑ _____ : _____

Ⓒ _____ : _____

Ⓓ _____ : _____

Correct answer: _____

Is your answer *class to member* or *member to class*? _____

Multiple-Meaning Words

Some words have more than one meaning. For example, the word *tire* can be a noun or a verb.

- A noun is a person, place or thing. (My bike has a flat <u>tire</u>.)
- A verb is an action word. (Did coach's practice <u>tire</u> you out?)

Directions: Fill in the circle next to the answer choice that best completes each analogy.

1. | It's around the <u>corner</u>. | : | The dogs will <u>corner</u> the cat. |

   Ⓐ noun : verb   Ⓑ verb : noun

2. | The <u>police</u> will help us. | : | <u>Police</u> the area for intruders. |

   Ⓐ noun : verb   Ⓑ verb : noun

3. | I'll <u>doctor</u> the photograph. | : | I need to see a <u>doctor</u>. |

   Ⓐ noun : verb   Ⓑ verb : noun

4. | Please don't <u>crowd</u> me. | : | The <u>crowd</u> waited patiently. |

   Ⓐ noun : verb   Ⓑ verb : noun

5. | It's easy to make a <u>mistake</u>. | : | People <u>mistake</u> me for Seth. |

   Ⓐ noun : verb   Ⓑ verb : noun

6. | <u>Signal</u> when you turn. | : | I will watch for your <u>signal</u>. |

   Ⓐ noun : verb   Ⓑ verb : noun

7. | We will <u>skate</u> at the rink. | : | My <u>skate</u> has a broken wheel. |

   Ⓐ noun : verb   Ⓑ verb : noun

8. | A <u>drill</u> is a tool. | : | Please <u>drill</u> me on my spelling words. |

   Ⓐ noun : verb   Ⓑ verb : noun

9. | Don't <u>fence</u> me in! | : | The <u>fence</u> needs paint. |

   Ⓐ noun : verb   Ⓑ verb : noun

10. | What is your <u>name</u>? | : | What will you <u>name</u> him? |

    Ⓐ noun : verb   Ⓑ verb : noun

Multiple-Meaning Words 2

Directions: Write out the connection between the word pair in the question. Then choose the answer that best completes each analogy. (**Hints:** Remember that some words have multiple meanings and watch out for which word comes first in the word pair.)

1. **paint : picture**
   - Ⓐ cake : frost
   - Ⓑ frost : cake
   - Ⓒ snow : white
   - Ⓓ white : snow

   You paint a picture.

2. **paint : liquid**
   - Ⓐ boil : water
   - Ⓑ water : boil
   - Ⓒ solid : ice
   - Ⓓ ice : solid

3. **store : aisles**
   - Ⓐ bookstore : buy
   - Ⓑ buy : bookstore
   - Ⓒ bookcase : shelves
   - Ⓓ shelves : bookcase

4. **store : save**
   - Ⓐ create : make
   - Ⓑ make : break
   - Ⓒ sew : needle
   - Ⓓ needle : sew

5. **smell : smoke**
   - Ⓐ house : room
   - Ⓑ apple : pea
   - Ⓒ catch : ball
   - Ⓓ purse : pocket

6. **smell : odor**
   - Ⓐ run : glide
   - Ⓑ photo : picture
   - Ⓒ bite : sleep
   - Ⓓ draw : pencil

7. **point : location**
   - Ⓐ box : wrap
   - Ⓑ boil : water
   - Ⓒ pencil : yellow
   - Ⓓ arc : curve

8. **point : aim**
   - Ⓐ find : discover
   - Ⓑ find : lose
   - Ⓒ find : keep
   - Ⓓ find : treasure

9. **whistle : blow**
   - Ⓐ violin : wood
   - Ⓑ piano : key
   - Ⓒ drum : march
   - Ⓓ guitar : strum

10. **whistle : tune**
    - Ⓐ sing : song
    - Ⓑ note : music
    - Ⓒ music : radio
    - Ⓓ rap : hip hop

11. **guard : watch**
    - Ⓐ bake : oven
    - Ⓑ sweep : broom
    - Ⓒ stir : mix
    - Ⓓ clean : dirty

12. **guard : prison**
    - Ⓐ hospital : doctor
    - Ⓑ teacher : school
    - Ⓒ store : clerk
    - Ⓓ farm : farmer

13. Write down two meanings for the word *fish*.

   _____

   _____

14. Make an analogy with the word *fish*.

   _____ : _____ :: _____ : _____

Math

Directions: The analogies below test your knowledge of prime numbers and divisible numbers. Choose the answer that best completes each analogy.

Helpful Hints

- Remember, a prime number is only divisible by itself and 1.
- Also, here are some tests to do to check for divisibility:

Divisible by	If	Example
2	ends in 0, 2, 4, 6, 8	all even numbers
3	sum of digits is divisible by 3	243 (2 + 4 + 3 = 9)
4	last two digits are 00 or divisible by 4	2512 (12 is divisible by 4)
5	ends in 0 or 5	445
10	ends in 0	1,970

1. **prime : 17 :: prime :** _____

   (A) 12   (B) 29   (C) 93   (D) 110

2. **50 : 2, 5, 10 :: 55 :** _____

   (A) 2, 5, 10   (B) 2, 5   (C) 5, 10   (D) 5

3. **3,252 : 2, 3, 4 :: 6,513 :** _____

   (A) 2, 3, 4   (B) 2, 3   (C) 3   (D) prime

4. **3, 5, 10 : 90 :: 3, 4, 5, 10 :** _____

   (A) 600   (B) 525   (C) 410   (D) 365

5. **52 : 1, 2, 4, 52 :: 53 :** _____

   (A) 1, 2, 4, 53   (B) 1, 4, 53   (C) 1, 53   (D) 53

6. **2, 3 : 5, 7 :: 11, 13 :** _____

   (A) 17, 19   (B) 19, 21   (C) 23, 27   (D) 31, 35

7. **3 : 76134 :: 4 :** _____

   (A) 76133   (B) 76132   (C) 76131   (D) 76130

8. **one of many odd primes : only even prime :: 97 :** _____

   (A) 96   (B) 66   (C) 42   (D) 2

Challenge: Make your own math analogy using prime numbers or numbers divisible by 2, 3, 4, 5, and 10. Be prepared to explain your analogy.

_____ : _____ :: _____ : _____

Math 2

Directions: Use the information about triangles to help you answer the analogies.

- The three angles in a triangle must add up to 180°.
- The formula for finding the area of a triangle is $\frac{1}{2}$ base x height.
- There are several types of triangles:

 equilateral *three equal sides*

 isosceles *at least 2 equal sides*

 scalene *no equal sides*

 right *one 90° angle*

 acute *all angles < 90°*

 obtuse *one angle > 90°*

---

1. **right angle : 90° :: obtuse angle : _____**

   Ⓐ 18°   Ⓑ 68°   Ⓒ 118°   Ⓓ 89°

2. **180° : 32°, 65°, 83° :: 180° : _____**

   Ⓐ 45°,50°, 85°   Ⓑ 55°,75°, 100°   Ⓒ 9°,106°, 50°   Ⓓ 15°, 25°, 30°

3. **60°, 60°, 60° : equilateral :: 30°, 60°, 90° : _____**

   Ⓐ acute   Ⓑ obtuse   Ⓒ scalene   Ⓓ right

4. **two equal sides : isosceles :: no equal sides : _____**

   Ⓐ right   Ⓑ scalene   Ⓒ obtuse   Ⓓ equilateral

5. **obtuse angle : 91° :: acute angle : _____**

   Ⓐ 121°   Ⓑ 101°   Ⓒ 91°   Ⓓ 81°

6. **14°, 78° : 88° :: 33°, 18° :**

   Ⓐ 116°   Ⓑ 129°   Ⓒ 138°   Ⓓ 147°

7. **area of [triangle 3,4] : 6 :: area of [triangle 6,8] : _____**

   Ⓐ 12   Ⓑ 96   Ⓒ 24   Ⓓ 132

8. **20 : area of [triangle 4,10] :: 60 : area of [triangle ?,20]**

   Ⓐ 1   Ⓑ 3   Ⓒ 5   Ⓓ 6

Social Studies

Every state in the United States has a capital city where its government meets. The United States itself has a capital district.

Directions: Find the place name that best completes each analogy. (**Hint:** You may want to use an atlas, an almanac, or the Internet to find a map of the United States.)

1. Nebraska : Lincoln :: New York : _____

2. Alabama : Montgomery :: Texas : _____

3. Idaho : Boise :: California : _____

4. Delaware : Dover :: Colorado : _____

5. Nevada : Carson City :: Florida : _____

6. West Virginia : Charleston :: Virginia : _____

7. Columbus : Columbia :: Ohio : _____

8. Little Rock : Salem :: Arkansas : _____

9. Hartford : Harrisburg :: Connecticut : _____

10. Springfield : Lansing :: Illinois : _____

11. Kansas : Kentucky :: Topeka : _____

12. Minnesota : Indiana :: St. Paul : _____

13. Pierre : Bismarck :: South Dakota : _____

14. Oklahoma City : Jefferson City :: Oklahoma : _____

15. Olympia : Washington :: Washington, D.C. : _____

Challenge: Write an analogy of your own. Use different states and city names from the ones in the questions.

_____ : _____ :: _____ : _____

Social Studies 2

Directions: Write down the direction (north, south, east, west) that best completes each analogy. If needed, use an atlas or the Internet to do research.

Hint: Answers will depend on the direction each state is located from the geographical feature. For example, | **Mississippi River : Utah :: east : west** | . (The Mississippi River is east of Utah, and Utah is west of the Mississippi River.)

1. Lake Michigan : Wisconsin :: east : _____

2. Rocky Mountains : Massachusetts :: west : _____

3. Great Salt Lake : Iowa :: west : _____

4. Colorado River : Montana :: south : _____

5. Tennessee : Lake Huron :: south : _____

6. Missouri River : Texas :: north : _____

7. Appalachian Mountains : east :: Nevada : _____

8. South Dakota : Rio Grande River :: north : _____

9. Mount McKinley (Denali) : Mauna Kea :: north : _____

10. Lake Erie : New York :: west : _____

11. Mississippi River : Wyoming :: east : _____

12. Indiana : Lake Superior :: south : _____

Challenge: Write your own analogy using your state name or a geographical feature in it.

_____ : _____ :: _____ : _____

Science

Sunlight is known as visible or white light. Sunlight is a mixture of all visible colors. When sunlight passes through water droplets, it is bent and split into the colors of the rainbow. The order of the colors is always in the same order as the visible light spectrum.

A *mnemonic device* is an aid that helps you remember something. A common mnemonic for remembering the order of colors is the name **Roy G. Biv**.

Directions: Use the mnemonic **Roy G. Biv** to answer the analogies correctly.

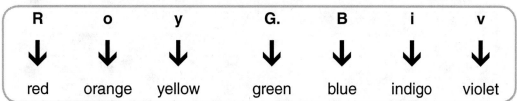

1. **R** is to **red** as **G** is to _____.

   Ⓐ orange   Ⓑ green   Ⓒ indigo   Ⓓ violet

2. **Y** is to **yellow** as **I** is to _____.

   Ⓐ green   Ⓑ orange   Ⓒ red   Ⓓ indigo

3. **Orange** is to **second** as **blue** is to _____.

   Ⓐ fifth   Ⓑ fourth   Ⓒ third   Ⓓ second

4. **First** is to **R** as **last** is to _____.

   Ⓐ v   Ⓑ y   Ⓒ G   Ⓓ i

5. **Indigo** is to **B** as **green** is to _____.

   Ⓐ o   Ⓑ R   Ⓒ y   Ⓓ B

6. **V** is to **blue** as **y** is to _____.

   Ⓐ green   Ⓑ indigo   Ⓒ orange   Ⓓ red

7. **Green** is to **before blue** as **o** is to _____.

   Ⓐ after violet   Ⓑ after yellow   Ⓒ after R   Ⓓ after i

8. **red**, **orange**, **yellow** is to **ROY** as **blue**, **indigo**, **violet** is to _____.

   Ⓐ Vib   Ⓑ Biv   Ⓒ ivb   Ⓓ Bvi

Challenge: Make up your own silly or serious mnemonic for the visible light spectrum.

    R   O   Y   G   B   I   V

_____ _____ _____ _____ _____ _____ _____

Science 2

Directions: Complete the analogies by using the weight chart for the planets (and the dwarf planet Pluto) in our solar system.

Planet	No. from Sun	W (weight per 100 lbs. on Earth)	Your Weight on Planet
Mercury	1	38	W x .38
Venus	2	90	W x .90
Earth	3	100	W x 1
Mars	4	38	W x .38
Jupiter	5	236	W x 2.36
Saturn	6	92	W x .92
Uranus	7	89	W x .89
Neptune	8	113	W x 1.13
Pluto	9	7	W x .07

1. **Heaviest** is to **lightest** as **Jupiter** is to _____.

   Ⓐ Venus Ⓑ Neptune Ⓒ Pluto Ⓓ Earth

2. **W x 1** is to **Earth** as **W x .89** is to _____.

   Ⓐ Uranus Ⓑ Mercury Ⓒ Saturn Ⓓ Jupiter

3. **38** is to **7** as **first** is to _____.

   Ⓐ second Ⓑ fourth Ⓒ sixth Ⓓ last

4. **Fourth** is to **W x .38** as **fifth** is to _____.

   Ⓐ W x 1 Ⓑ W x .92 Ⓒ W x 1.13 Ⓓ W x 2.36

5. **Earth** is to **200 pounds** as **Venus** is to _____.

   Ⓐ 90 pounds Ⓑ 120 pounds Ⓒ 160 pounds Ⓓ 180 pounds

6. **38** is to **100** as **236** is to _____.

   Ⓐ 89 Ⓑ 7 Ⓒ 113 Ⓓ 38

7. **Pluto** is to **3.5 pounds** as **Uranus** is to _____.

   Ⓐ 44 pounds Ⓑ 44.5 pounds Ⓒ 178 pounds Ⓓ 178.5 pounds

8. **W x 1.13** is to **eighth** as **W x .38** is to _____.

   Ⓐ second Ⓑ third Ⓒ fourth Ⓓ fifth

Think and Write: Would one weigh more or less on Earth's moon than on the dwarf planet Pluto? (**Hint:** Earth's moon is slightly larger than Pluto.)

Skeleton Analogies

Directions: Use the cat skeleton to help you complete each analogy.

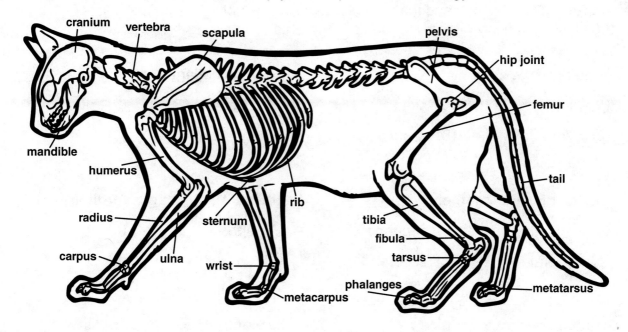

1. back leg : femur :: front leg : _____

2. forepaw : metacarpus :: hindpaw : _____

3. ulna : radius :: fibula : _____

4. wrist : carpus :: ankle : _____

5. ribs : chest :: cranium : _____

6. jawbone : shoulder blade :: mandible : _____

7. breastbone : sternum :: hip bone : _____

8. thigh : femur :: toe : _____

Challenge: Who do you think has more bones: a person or a cat? Tell why you think so.

_____

_____

Spelling

Directions: Use your spelling skills and/or a dictionary to complete the analogies.
(**Be careful:** the underlined and the correct answer words below are on many lists of the "100 Most Commonly Misspelled Words in the English Language"!)

1. none : <u>no one</u> :: many : _____
   - Ⓐ alot
   - Ⓒ alote
   - Ⓑ a lot
   - Ⓓ allot

2. poor : <u>excellent</u> :: similar : _____
   - Ⓐ diferant
   - Ⓒ diferent
   - Ⓑ differant
   - Ⓓ different

3. whole : <u>piece</u> :: together : _____
   - Ⓐ saperate
   - Ⓒ separate
   - Ⓑ seperate
   - Ⓓ seperete

4. pleasure : <u>business</u> :: ordinary : _____
   - Ⓐ special
   - Ⓒ speshell
   - Ⓑ specail
   - Ⓓ spesial

5. needed : <u>necessary</u> :: nice : _____
   - Ⓐ pleesant
   - Ⓒ pleasant
   - Ⓑ pleasent
   - Ⓓ plesant

6. barbecued : <u>barbecue</u> :: lost : _____
   - Ⓐ lose
   - Ⓒ loos
   - Ⓑ loose
   - Ⓓ luce

7. strange : <u>weird</u> : smart : _____
   - Ⓐ jenius
   - Ⓒ genuous
   - Ⓑ genous
   - Ⓓ genius

8. show : <u>camouflage</u> :: rest : _____
   - Ⓐ exersise
   - Ⓒ exersize
   - Ⓑ exercise
   - Ⓓ exercize

9. last : <u>finally</u> :: start : _____
   - Ⓐ begining
   - Ⓒ beginning
   - Ⓑ beganing
   - Ⓓ beganning

10. happen : <u>occur</u> :: capture : _____
    - Ⓐ seize
    - Ⓒ seeze
    - Ⓑ sieze
    - Ⓓ seaze

11. Pick one of the most commonly misspelled words. Why is it easy or difficult for you to spell?

_____

_____

Challenge: On the back of this paper, write one sentence with as many of the most commonly misspelled words as you can. Make sure the words are spelled correctly!

Homophones

Homophones are words that sound alike. Homophones are not spelled the same, and they have different meanings.

Directions: Give three reasons why *not* and *knot* are homophones.

1. _____

2. _____

3. _____

Directions: Pick the correct homophone from the word box to complete the analogies.

their	principle	they're	reign
there	rain	principal	rein

1. city : mayor :: school : _____

2. ox : yoke :: horse : _____

3. own : borrow :: our : _____

4. free : release :: rule : _____

5. right : here :: over : _____

6. basic lie : falsehood :: basic truth : _____

7. is not : isn't :: they are : _____

8. flake : snow :: drop : _____

9. Circle the correct spelling for the word that means the head of a school. Underline the part of the word (three letters) that helps you remember. (**Hint:** The head of your school is your friend.)

principle   principal

Challenge: Can you think of homophones for each of the words in the first word pair in question 5?

• right: _____   • here: _____

Homophones 2

Homophones are words that sound alike. Homophones are not spelled the same, and they have different meanings.

Directions: Give three reasons why *guessed* and *guest* are homophones.

1. _____

2. _____

3. _____

Directions: Pick the correct homophone from the word box to complete the analogies.

ball	break	forth	lesson
bawl	brake	fourth	lessen

1. first : second :: third : _____

2. smile : grin :: cry : _____

3. rise : increase :: lower : _____

4. house : castle :: dance : _____

5. mend : repair :: destroy : _____

6. retreat : back :: advance : _____

7. eat : consume :: stop : _____

8. read : book :: learn : _____

Directions: Rewrite the sentences with the correct word spellings.

9. Lettuce now prays famous men. _____

10. Eye no ewe wood like two eat this juicy stake. _____

_____

Think and Write: Explain why spelling is important, even if one has a spell check on a computer. Use the word *homophone* in your answer.

_____

_____

Fun with Presidents

Directions: Find out presidential facts by answering the analogies.

Hint: You may want to find a list that names the presidents in order before you start.

1. Said, "We have nothing to fear but fear itself." (32nd) **:** Said, "Ask not what your country can do for you. Ask what you can do for your country." (35th) **::**

   _____ **:** _____

2. only bachelor elected (15th) **:** only president married in the White House (22nd, 24th) **::**

   _____ **:** _____

3. shortest time in office—one month (9th) **:** longest time in office—almost 13 years (32nd) **::**

   _____ **:** _____

4. last president born in log cabin (20th) **:** president born in last state to join the Union (44th) **::**

   _____ **:** _____

5. president and son of a president (6th) **:** president and father of a president (41st) **::**

   _____ **:** _____

6. president who ran unopposed both terms (1st) **:** president who ran unopposed second term (5th) **::**

   _____ **:** _____

7. first to live in the White House (2nd) **:** first to have running water in the White House (13th) **::**

   _____ **:** _____

8. first to ride a train (7th) **:** first to be born in a hospital (39th) **::**

   _____ **:** _____

Challenge: The 8th president was the first president to be born a U.S. citizen. Who was the 8th president, and why do you think the previous seven weren't born U.S. citizens?

_____

_____

Fearful Analogies

Directions: Don't be afraid! If you use the chart, you will be able to complete the analogies correctly. A *phobia* is a very strong and unreasonable fear.

Phobia	Fear of
zoophobia	animals
hippophobia	horses
hydrophobia	water
acrophobia	heights
microphobia	small things

Phobia	Fear of
ergophobia	work
potamophobia	rivers
xenophobia	strangers
arachnophobia	spiders
triskaidekaphobia	the number 13

1. **Indian Ocean : hydrophobia**
   - Ⓐ best friend : xenophobia
   - Ⓑ xenophobia : best friend
   - Ⓒ Nile River : potamophobia
   - Ⓓ potamophobia : Nile River

2. **ergophobia : toil**
   - Ⓐ gorilla : zoophobia
   - Ⓑ zoophobia : gorilla
   - Ⓒ hippopotamus : hippophobia
   - Ⓓ hippophonia : hippopotamus

3. **acrophobia : mountain top**
   - Ⓐ triskaidekaphobia : 13
   - Ⓑ triskaidekaphobia : 23
   - Ⓒ triskaidekaphobia : 33
   - Ⓓ triskaidekaphobia : 43

4. **miniscule bits : microphobia**
   - Ⓐ anacondas : arachnophobia
   - Ⓑ gazelles : arachnophobia
   - Ⓒ vultures : arachnophobia
   - Ⓓ tarantulas : arachnophobia

5. **newcomer : xenophobia**
   - Ⓐ cage : zoophobia
   - Ⓑ Lake Erie : potamophobia
   - Ⓒ stallion : hippophobia
   - Ⓓ castle : microphobia

6. **arachnophobia : Black Widow**
   - Ⓐ zoophobia : fern
   - Ⓑ ergophobia : rest
   - Ⓒ triskaidekaphobia : 3
   - Ⓓ xenophobia : foreigner

7. **climbing : acrophobia**
   - Ⓐ bathing : hydrophobia
   - Ⓑ playing : ergophobia
   - Ⓒ studying : potamophobia
   - Ⓓ building : xenophobia

8. **triskaidekaphobia : 5**
   - Ⓐ arachnophobia : Brown Recluse spider
   - Ⓑ zoophobia : heights
   - Ⓒ potamophobia : Amazon River
   - Ⓓ hippophobia : colt

9. When the hippopotamus was named, two Greek words were used: *hippos* and *potamos*. What do you think these two words mean?

   • Hippos: _____   • potamos: _____

10. Based on the information you have learned, what do you think is the source of *hydroelectric* power?

Extreme Analogies

Directions: Find out extreme nature facts by answering the analogies. (**Note:** Some of this information may be completely new to you. You may need to look up information in books or on the Internet. If it is okay with your teacher, groups of students can find the answers to just some of the questions. Then each group can share what they learned with the class.)

1. **smallest ocean : largest :: Arctic :**

   Ⓐ Atlantic   Ⓑ Coral   Ⓒ Pacific   Ⓓ Indian

2. **smallest mammal : largest :: Kitti's hog-nosed bat :**

   Ⓐ elephant   Ⓑ giraffe   Ⓒ beluga whale   Ⓓ blue whale

3. **smallest bird : largest :: bee hummingbird :**

   Ⓐ bald eagle   Ⓑ ostrich   Ⓒ buzzard   Ⓓ emu

4. **deepest lake : longest river :: Lake Baikal :**

   Ⓐ Amazon   Ⓑ Mississippi   Ⓒ Yangtze   Ⓓ Nile

5. **oldest tree : largest :: bristlecone pine :**

   Ⓐ giant sequoia   Ⓑ redwood   Ⓒ oak   Ⓓ cedar

6. **smallest flower : largest :: watermeal :**

   Ⓐ rose   Ⓑ rafflesia   Ⓒ peony   Ⓓ daffodil

7. **longest snake : biggest (heaviest) :: reticulated python :**

   Ⓐ mamba   Ⓑ rattlesnake   Ⓒ anaconda   Ⓓ cobra

8. **fastest land bird : flying :: ostrich :**

   Ⓐ peregrine falcon   Ⓑ harpy eagle   Ⓒ swift   Ⓓ kiwi

9. **fastest animal : slowest :: cheetah :**

   Ⓐ tortoise   Ⓑ ant   Ⓒ sloth   Ⓓ mule

10. **longest insect : invertebrate :: Giant Walking Stick :**

    Ⓐ jellyfish   Ⓑ octopus   Ⓒ mollusk   Ⓓ colossal squid

Challenge: Find more information on your own about one of nature's extremes using books or the Internet. On a separate piece of paper, write down five facts.

Review of Analogy Types

Directions: Choose the answer that best completes each analogy. Write **synonyms**, **antonyms**, **plural**, **adjective**, **what people use**, or **past/present** on the blank line to describe how the question and answer words are connected. (**Hint:** There will be two of each kind of analogy.) Remember to pay attention to order!

1. **soup : warm**
   - Ⓐ frozen : ice
   - Ⓑ peel : apple
   - Ⓒ popsicle : cold
   - Ⓓ stir : lemon

2. **inspect : ignore**
   - Ⓐ display : hide
   - Ⓑ droop : sag
   - Ⓒ drench : wet
   - Ⓓ damage : harm

3. **blew : blow**
   - Ⓐ stand : stood
   - Ⓑ leave : left
   - Ⓒ steal : stole
   - Ⓓ thought : think

4. **grouchy : cranky**
   - Ⓐ young : ancient
   - Ⓑ wicked : evil
   - Ⓒ wealthy : poor
   - Ⓓ gloomy : merry

5. **fisherman : rod**
   - Ⓐ referee : whistle
   - Ⓑ oven : baker
   - Ⓒ tire : bicycle
   - Ⓓ tractor : farmer

6. **house : houses**
   - Ⓐ children : child
   - Ⓑ stories : story
   - Ⓒ mouse : mice
   - Ⓓ rockets : rocket

7. **snatch : grab**
   - Ⓐ enjoy : hate
   - Ⓑ search : seek
   - Ⓓ show : cover
   - Ⓒ stretch : squish

8. **athlete : fit**
   - Ⓐ round : ball
   - Ⓑ elastic : stretchy
   - Ⓒ square : block
   - Ⓓ heavy : brick

9. **rake : gardener**
   - Ⓐ runner : helmet
   - Ⓑ teacher : chalk
   - Ⓒ janitor : mop
   - Ⓓ needle : tailor

10. **city : cities**
    - Ⓐ half : halves
    - Ⓑ wife : wifes
    - Ⓒ baby : babys
    - Ⓓ man : mans

11. **agree : disagree**
    - Ⓐ usual : regular
    - Ⓑ wail : cry
    - Ⓒ catch : release
    - Ⓓ admire : like

12. **burst : burst**
    - Ⓐ greet : greeted
    - Ⓑ sing : sang
    - Ⓒ take : took
    - Ⓓ wound : wind

13. Why did you have to eliminate answer choices to find the correct answer for question 12?

Review of Analogy Types 2

Directions: Choose the answer that best completes each analogy. Write **homophones**, **purpose**, **where found**, **member to group**, **less/more**, or **male/female** on the blank line to describe how the question and answer words are connected. (**Hint:** There will be two of each kind of analogy.) Remember to pay attention to order!

1. **cherry : fruit**
   - (A) mammal : cat
   - (B) furniture : desk
   - (C) tree : redwood
   - (D) football : game

2. **ask : beg**
   - (A) talk : word
   - (B) talk : shout
   - (C) talk : answer
   - (D) talk : listen

3. **peace : piece**
   - (A) hour : our
   - (B) bait : beat
   - (C) know : knee
   - (D) phone : police

4. **book : library**
   - (A) tiger : stripes
   - (B) rodent : mouse
   - (C) animal : zoo
   - (D) star : spaceship

5. **eye : observe**
   - (A) nose : face
   - (B) scale : weigh
   - (C) bowl : spoon
   - (D) call : phone

6. **scene : seen**
   - (A) sail : sailed
   - (B) stare : steak
   - (C) ship : send
   - (D) shown : shone

7. **nephew : niece**
   - (A) duchess : duke
   - (B) princess : prince
   - (C) uncle : aunt
   - (D) lady : lord

8. **bull : cow**
   - (A) doe : buck
   - (B) mare : stallion
   - (C) lion : lioness
   - (D) hen : rooster

9. **microscope : lab**
   - (A) dishwasher : kitchen
   - (B) sink : living room
   - (C) mirror : forest
   - (D) penguin : desert

10. **swallow : gulp**
    - (A) jump : rope
    - (B) jog : race
    - (C) shoe : sock
    - (D) shake : milk

11. **summer : season**
    - (A) Monday : weekend
    - (B) month : Friday
    - (C) year : July
    - (D) Tuesday : weekday

12. **spade : dig**
    - (A) broom : sweep
    - (B) chop : axe
    - (C) measure : ruler
    - (D) nail : hammer

13. If the wrong answers for question 12 had been written in a different order, would they have been correct?

Use What You Know

Sometimes you may not know a word. Don't give up! Sometimes you can figure out the answer by using what you know.

Directions: Go through the answer choices. Write down how the words you know are connected. Cross out the ones that do not have the same connection as the words in the question. The correct answer will be the one that is not crossed out.

Connection

1. **polluted : clean**   antonyms

    Ⓐ eagle : bird   not antonyms, member to group

    Ⓑ incorrect : wrong

    Ⓒ ludicrous : serious   ?????

    Ⓓ paint : brush

2. **Most likely, something *ludicrous* is**

    Ⓐ enormous   Ⓑ not enormous   Ⓒ ridiculous   Ⓓ not ridiculous

Connection

3. **pat : stroke**

    Ⓐ doff : remove   ?????

    Ⓑ mend : rip

    Ⓒ drink : glass

    Ⓓ travel : remain

4. **Most likely, when one *doffs* something, one**

    Ⓐ puts it on   Ⓑ removes it   Ⓒ touches it   Ⓓ doesn't touch it

5. First, look up the words *ludicrous* and *doff* in the dictionary. Write down what they mean.

    • ludicrous: _____

    • doff: _____

Next, rewrite the following sentences on the back of this paper, but substitute *ludicrous* or *doff* for the underlined words.

    • Grandma says that when a man enters a room, he should always <u>remove</u> his hat.

    • I think 10" heels are <u>ridiculous</u>; they look as silly as they are dangerous.

On the back of this paper, use the words *ludicrous* and *doff* in two sentences of your own.

Use What You Know 2

Directions: Go through the answer choices. Write down how the words you know are connected. Cross out the ones that do not have the same connection as the words in the question. The correct answer will be the one that is not crossed out.

Connection

1. **deer : doe** _____

   Ⓐ hen : chick _____

   Ⓑ sheep : lamb _____

   Ⓒ cow : calf _____

   Ⓓ donkey : jenny _____

2. **Most likely, a *jenny* is a**

   Ⓐ baby donkey   Ⓑ male swan   Ⓒ female donkey   Ⓓ group of donkeys

Connection

3. **kitten : cat** _____

   Ⓐ hatchling : crocodile _____

   Ⓑ chicken : rooster _____

   Ⓒ horse : stallion _____

   Ⓓ pig : boar

4. **Most likely, a *hatchling* is a**

   Ⓐ baby crocodile   Ⓑ male crocodile   Ⓒ female crocodile   Ⓓ group of crocodiles

5. **mountaineer : mountain**

   Ⓐ water : scuba diver

   Ⓑ track : racer

   Ⓒ spelunker : cave

   Ⓓ waves : surfer

6. **pool : swimmer**

   Ⓐ soccer player : field

   Ⓑ actor : stage

   Ⓒ chef : restaurant

   Ⓓ air : aerialist

7. **Most likely, a *spelunker***

   Ⓐ fears caves

   Ⓑ explores caves

   Ⓒ is a large cave

   Ⓓ makes caves

8. **Most likely, an *aerialist* performs**

   Ⓐ high off the ground

   Ⓑ blindfolded

   Ⓒ on the ground

   Ⓓ without a blindfold

Challenge: Find out more information on spelunkers and aerialists using books or the Internet. Tell which activity you would be most likely to engage in and why. Use the back of this paper.

Use What You Know 3

Directions: Read all the answer choices. Think about how the words are connected. **If the words in the answer choices are connected in the same way, they cannot be the answer!** This is because there is only one correct answer.

Connection

1. *unknown word : unknown word*

   Ⓐ ludicrous : ridiculous _____synonyms_____

   Ⓑ doffs : removes _____

   Ⓒ detest : love _____

   Ⓓ spelunker : caver _____

   Answer choices _____, _____, and _____ must be wrong because they are all _____. The correct answer is _____.

Connection

2. *unknown word : unknown word*

   Ⓐ stationary : stationery _____

   Ⓑ limp : hobble _____

   Ⓒ sight : site _____

   Ⓓ principal : principle _____

   Answer choices _____, _____, and _____ must be wrong because they are all _____. The correct answer is _____.

Connection

3. *unknown word : unknown word*

   Ⓐ refrigerator : cool _____

   Ⓑ oven : bake _____

   Ⓒ freezer : freeze _____

   Ⓓ fork : silverware _____

   Answer choices _____, _____, and _____ must be wrong because they are all _____. The correct answer is _____.

4. Write down four pairs of answer choices. Make three of them the same link. See if a classmate can tell you what the right answer is!

   Ⓐ _____ : _____   Ⓒ _____ : _____

   Ⓑ _____ : _____   Ⓓ _____ : _____

Use What You Know 4

Directions: Read all the answer choices. Think about how the words are connected. **If the words in the answer choices are connected in the same way, they cannot be the answer!** This is because there is only one correct answer.

Connection

1. *unknown word : unknown word*

   Ⓐ emperor : empress _____

   Ⓑ lord : castle _____

   Ⓒ king : queen _____

   Ⓓ duke : duchess _____

   Answer choices _____, _____, and _____ must be wrong because they are all

   _____. The correct answer is _____.

2. *unknown : unknown*

   Ⓐ attic : loft

   Ⓑ cellar : basement

   Ⓒ study : den

   Ⓓ living room : kitchen

3. *unknown : unknown*

   Ⓐ tie : shoes

   Ⓑ scarf : wrap

   Ⓒ zip : jacket

   Ⓓ button : shirt

4. **August : month**

   Ⓐ Monday : day

   Ⓑ minute : second

   Ⓒ week : day

   Ⓓ month : week

5. *august : noble*

   Ⓐ delicious : flavorless

   Ⓑ shy : outgoing

   Ⓒ energetic : active

   Ⓓ interesting : boring

6. The noun *August* is the name of a _____.

7. The adjective *august* is used to describe someone who is _____ or someone who causes one to feel awe and respect.

8. *Augustus* is a Latin adjective that describes one as worthy of respect, or exalted. The month of August was named for the Roman emperor Augustus Caesar. How do you think people felt about Augustus Caesar? _____

9. If someone said, "He is an august judge," is the judge being complimented? Explain why or why not. _____

_____

Analogies in Writing

Directions: Think of a rock. Then, think of a person. Write down two ways a person might be thought of like a rock.

1. _____

2. _____

An analogy is a likeness in some ways between things that are otherwise unlike. Writers often use analogies to help the reader make pictures in their heads.

Directions: For #3–6, choose the set of words that best completes this sentence:

If a writer compares a person to a rock, the writer may want the reader to make a picture in his

or her head of a _____.

3. (A) strong person

   (B) weak person

4. (A) *feeble* person (weak, frail, unconvincing)

   (B) *stalwart* person (strong, well-built, brave, firm)

5. (A) person who always follows the crowd

   (B) person who makes up his or her own mind

6. (A) person who can be depended on

   (B) person who cannot be depended on

7. Make an analogy where you compare yourself, a person from history, or a person from a book (real or make-believe) to an inanimate item. (If something is inanimate, it is not living.) Use the words *feeble* and *stalwart* in your answer. Use complete sentences.

_____ : _____
      (person)   *(inanimate item)*

_____ is/am a _____ because _____

_____

_____

_____

_____

Analogies in Writing 2

Remember, an **analogy** is a likeness in some ways between things that are otherwise unlike.

Directions: Complete the sentence and write more sentences to finish each analogy. Make sure you use lots of descriptive words to help the reader make a picture in his or her head.

1. The thief was like an eel because _____

    _____

    _____

2. A child is like a clean slate because _____

    _____

    _____

3. A super athlete's life is like an open book because _____

    _____

    _____

4. Antarctica is like a separate planet because _____

    _____

    _____

5. Taking a photograph is like freezing time because _____

    _____

    _____

6. Ending a friendship is like closing a door because _____

    _____

    _____

7. An airport is like a beehive because _____

    _____

    _____

8. A _____ is like a _____ because _____

    _____

    _____

Share one of your analogies with the class.

Far Out Analogies

Directions: Think outside the box! Make up analogies that are so far out that the only adjective that can be used to describe them is "ludicrous."

- **Example 1:** elephant : refrigerator :: python : closet
- **Link:** You don't expect to find or see an elephant in your refrigerator, just as you don't expect to find or see a python in your closet!
- **Example 2:** chocolate cake : ketchup :: ice cream : pepper
- **Link:** Chocolate cake isn't topped with ketchup, just as ice cream isn't topped with pepper.

---

1. **spider : ten :: horse :** _____

    • **Link:** _____

    _____

2. **Uranus : house :: Venus :** _____

    • **Link:** _____

    _____

3. **ride : hornet :: build :** _____

    • **Link:** _____

    _____

4. **enormous : mouse ::** _____ **:** _____

    • **Link:** _____

    _____

5. **computer : lake ::** _____ **:** _____

    • **Link:** _____

    _____

6. _____ **:** _____ **as** _____ **:** _____

    • **Link:** _____

    _____

7. _____ **:** _____ **as** _____ **:** _____

    • **Link:** _____

    _____

Read one of your analogies to your classmates. Could anyone figure out the link?

Analogies in Reading

Directions: Read the passage. Answer the questions.

"Jean Francois Gravelot isn't human. He's part spider," Lara said.

"What do you mean?" asked Jake. "How can a man be part spider?"

"When he acts like a spider," answered Lara. "Gravelot was a French aerialist. He was the first person to cross Niagara Falls on a tightrope. In 1859, he crossed on a 3-inch (7.6 cm) rope. In the middle, he stopped and drank some water from the Niagara River! How did he get the water? By dropping a bottle tied to a rope into the raging torrent below him!

"One time he crossed the falls on a bicycle. Another time he swung by one arm, turned somersaults, and stood on his head on a chair. He's crossed on stilts, blindfolded, and most amazing of all, once carrying someone on his back!"

"He's like a spider," laughed Jake, "but you can bet that the man he carried on his back was more like a terrified leech!"

Niagara Falls

1. **The analogy between Gravelot and a spider works because Gravelot**

   Ⓐ studied spiders before walking a tightrope.

   Ⓑ is as skillful as a spider on a thin web strand.

2. **Jake said the man Gravelot carried was analogous to a leech because both the man and the leech**

   Ⓐ suck blood from other creatures.

   Ⓑ attach themselves tightly to another creature.

3. **Both Gravelot and the man he carried must have had great trust in each other. Tell why.**

   _____

   _____

   _____

Challenge: Look in books or on the Internet to find out more about Jean Francois Gravelot.

Analogies in Reading 2

Directions: Read the passage. Answer the questions.

Lynne Cox is analogous to a penguin. This is because she is the only person in the world to swim a mile to Antarctica. All she wore was an ordinary one-piece swimsuit and a bathing cap. When she tucked in her long hair and put on her cap, she made sure to leave a little space at the top. This way her hair could help keep her warm, like insulating penguin feathers, trapping warm air next to its skin.

Most people would have died from hypothermia. Cox swam for 25 minutes! More dangerous than the icebergs were the smaller pieces of floating ice. They were hard to spot, with edges as sharp as broken glass. If she hit one, she could be knocked unconscious or badly cut.

At one point, penguins dove in next to her. They swam inches from her hands. Cox welcomed them, as this meant there weren't any predators such as orcas or leopard seals in the area. When Cox finished, she was so cold her brain wasn't working properly. Her support crew huddled around. Just like with penguins, their combined body heat helped warm her.

1. **Which answer is not a reason why the analogy between Cox and a penguin works?**

   Ⓐ penguins swim

   Ⓑ penguins are predators

   Ⓒ penguins huddle around each other for warmth

   Ⓓ penguins use their feathers to trap insulating air

2. **Does comparing ice to broken glass help one to understand or picture some of the dangers Cox faced? Explain why or why not.**

   _____

   _____

   _____

   _____

   _____

Challenge: Find out more about Lynne Cox by looking in books or on the Internet.

Analogies in Reading 3

Directions: Read the passage. Answer the questions.

A scientist is like a detective. A detective's clues are like a scientist's observations. Both the detective and the scientist have to organize their clues. They have to decide how they fit together.

Sometimes, clues come unexpectedly. For example, one time, through an open window, some plant mold blew in and landed on some experimental jelly in a dish in Alexander Fleming's lab. Fleming didn't throw the dish away. He kept it, waiting to see what would happen. What was the result? The discovery of penicillin!

Discovering the drug was not enough. Scientists had to solve something. They had to figure out how to manufacture the drug. They had to manufacture it in a way that made it practical for human use. It wasn't until 13 years later that scientists cracked the case!

1. **The analogy in the story compares**

   (A) a clue to 13 years.

   (B) an open window to a jelly dish.

   (C) a scientist to a detective.

   (D) an observation to penicillin.

2. **Complete the analogies, using different inventions and inventors' names. You may find your answers in books or searching the Internet. Pay attention to what comes first, the name or the invention!**

   • penicillin : Fleming :: _____ : _____

   • passenger elevator : Otis :: _____ : _____

   • Knight : paper bag machine :: _____ : _____

   • De Mestral : Velcro :: _____ : _____

Challenge: Write one paragraph about one of the inventors and his or her invention that you used as an answer.

_____

_____

_____

_____

Connection Review

Directions: Look at the word pairs in the first column. Think about how they are connected. Match the word pairs in the first column with a phrase from the second column that tells how they are connected. The first one has been done for you.

Hints: Use each phrase only once. If you do not know an answer right away, skip it. Come back to it at the end.

Word Pairs	How They Are Connected
_____ J _____ 1. **spaceship** to **space**	**A.** antonym (opposite)
_____ 2. **curious : uninterested**	**B.** synonym (same meaning)
_____ 3. **understood : understand**	**C.** homophone (same sound)
_____ 4. **pause : paws**	**D.** multiple-meaning word
_____ 5. **beach : sandy**	**E.** adjective
_____ 6. **steward : stewardess**	**F.** classifying (group to member)
_____ 7. **ox : oxen**	**G.** past to present
_____ 8. **prank : joke**	**H.** one to more (plural)
_____ 9. **toss : turn**	**I.** purpose
_____ 10. **crowd : crowd**	**J.** where things go
_____ 11. **seismograph : earthquake**	**K.** things or words that go together
_____ 12. **ocean : Atlantic**	**L.** male to female

Challenge: Write two sentences. In each sentence use the multiple-meaning word from above in a different way.

1. _____

_____

2. _____

_____

Connection Review 2

Directions: Look at the word pairs in the first column. Think about how they are connected. Match the word pairs in the first column with a phrase from the second column that tells how they are connected. The first one has been done for you.

Hints: Use each phrase only once. If you do not know an answer right away, skip it. Come back to it at the end.

Word Pairs	How They Are Connected
_K_ 1. **slide : slippery**	A. antonym (opposite)
_____ 2. **breeze : tornado**	B. synonym (same meaning)
_____ 3. **corner : corner**	C. homophone (same sound)
_____ 4. **dissolve : melt**	D. less than/more than
_____ 5. **musician : instrument**	E. family names
_____ 6. **graceful : clumsy**	F. what people use
_____ 7. **porcupine : quills**	G. part name to animal
_____ 8. **plain : plane**	H. multiple-meaning word
_____ 9. **conductor : train**	I. outside or on top
_____ 10. **boar : pig**	J. classifying (member to group)
_____ 11. **Jupiter : planet**	K. adjective
_____ 12. **trunk : elephant**	L. where work

Challenge: Write two sentences. In each sentence use the multiple-meaning word from above in a different way.

1. _____

_____

2. _____

_____

Practice Being the Teacher

Directions: It is your turn to teach. Look at the word pair. Show how to find the answer to the analogy.

gather : assemble

(A) amuse : bore   (C) rescue : save

(B) chair : sit   (D) dine : starve

1. First, write out how the words in the box are connected.

   • When you _g_____, you _a_____.

   Next, try out the connection with the other word pairs.

   (A) When you _a_____, you _b_____.

   (B) When you _c_____, you _s_____.

   (C) When you _r_____, you _s_____.

   (D) When you _d_____, you _s_____.

2. Answers _____ and _____ cannot be right because they have the same connection. They are both _____. (*synonyms* or *antonyms*)

3. Answer _____ cannot be right because the words in the word pair are not _____. (*synonyms* or *antonyms*)

---

4. What would be the answer if the question was | **creep : crept** | ?

   (A) dug : dig   (C) heal : doctor

   (B) searched : search   (D) cost : cost

5. Answers _____ and _____ are wrong because the verb tense is written in the wrong order. It should be _____ *to* _____, not _____ *to* _____.

6. Answer _____ is wrong because the words are not connected in the same way. The word _h_____ is not the past tense of _____.

Practice Being the Teacher 2

Directions: It is your turn to teach. Look at the word pair. Show how to find the answer to the analogy.

> **telescope : spot**

(A) broke : poor   (C) connect : join

(B) cool : refrigerator   (D) sponge : wipe

1. First, write out how the words in the box are connected.

   • You use a _t_____ to _s_____ .

   Next, try out the connection with the other word pairs.

   (A) You use a _b_____ to _p_____ .

   (B) You use a _c_____ to _r_____ .

   (C) You use a _c_____ to _j_____ .

   (D) You use a _s_____ to _w_____ .

2. Answers _____ and _____ cannot be right because they have the same connection. They are both _____. (*synonyms* or *antonyms*)

3. Answer _____ cannot be right because it is in the wrong order.

4. What would be the answer if the question was | **chimpanzee : mammal** | ?

   (A) insect : cockroach   (C) rattlesnake : reptile

   (B) salamanders : amphibian   (D) bird : owl

5. Answer _____ is wrong because the first word is plural (more than one).

6. Answers _____ and _____ are wrong because they are written in the wrong order.

7. Write your own analogy question with answers. Only one answer choice should be correct. Explain how to solve your analogy to a classmate.

   _____ : _____

   (A) _____ : _____   (C) _____ : _____

   (B) _____ : _____   (D) _____ : _____

Practice What You Know

Directions: Find the answer that best completes each analogy. Remember to . . .

- pay attention to word order
- think about how the words are connected
- read every answer choice
- cross out the ones that can't be right.

1. sir : madam
- (A) Miss : Master
- (B) king : prince
- (C) Mister : Mrs.
- (D) duchess : duke

2. quarrel : argue
- (A) monkey : tail
- (B) draw : erase
- (C) multiply : divide
- (D) sample : taste

3. block : tower
- (A) wall : brick
- (B) cobblestone : street
- (C) fence : picket
- (D) chimney : stone

4. house : palace
- (A) pebble : boulder
- (B) ocean : puddle
- (C) truck : car
- (D) shack : thatch

5. letter : envelope
- (A) dish : soap
- (B) floor : ceiling
- (C) bucket : trash
- (D) toothpaste : tube

6. gaggle : geese
- (A) herd : buffalo
- (B) rabbit : hop
- (C) fish : school
- (D) octopus : eight

7. marry : merry
- (A) cheerful : wed
- (B) wed : cheerful
- (C) happy : none
- (D) none : happy

8. swept : sweep
- (A) mop : mopped
- (B) catch : caught
- (C) drank : drink
- (D) sell : sold

9. energetic : tired
- (A) clean : tidy
- (B) depart : leave
- (C) fuzzy : smooth
- (D) delicious : tasty

10. lemon : tart
- (A) rose : fragrant
- (B) smooth : glass
- (C) sandy : beach
- (D) flat : plain

11. dog : beagle
- (A) mouse : pest
- (B) bird : parakeet
- (C) cat : meow
- (D) pansy : flower

12. word : letter
- (A) page : book
- (B) vowel : number
- (C) author : title
- (D) paragraph : sentence

13. Make an analogy with the country you live in and its capital. Use other country and city names for answer choices. Only one answer should be correct.

_____ : _____
(your country)   (your capital)

- (A) _____ : _____
- (B) _____ : _____
- (C) _____ : _____
- (D) _____ : _____

14. Which answer is correct? _____ Why? _____

_____

Practice What You Know 2

Directions: Find the answer that best completes each analogy. Remember to . . .

- pay attention to word order
- think about how the words are connected
- read every answer choice
- cross out the ones that can't be right.

1. **tree : branch**
   - (A) root : fern
   - (B) thorn : rose
   - (C) tiger : stripe
   - (D) monkey : arm

2. **wolves : wolf**
   - (A) women : woman
   - (B) dog : barks
   - (C) ants : picnic
   - (D) cuts : slice

3. **alarm : warn**
   - (A) clock : tick
   - (B) horse : neigh
   - (C) axe : chop
   - (D) phone : ringtone

4. **cat : prowls**
   - (A) giraffe : neck
   - (B) moth : flutters
   - (C) puppy : litter
   - (D) fish : tastes

5. **attic : house**
   - (A) loft : barn
   - (B) gate : open
   - (C) castle : moat
   - (D) floor : ceiling

6. **desire : want**
   - (A) smash : fix
   - (B) plot : plan
   - (C) transmit : receive
   - (D) organize : mix

7. **top : spins**
   - (A) paddle : canoe
   - (B) carrot : ground
   - (C) ball : bounces
   - (D) catch : mitt

8. **crack : canyon**
   - (A) river : stream
   - (B) sand : dune
   - (C) wave : swell
   - (D) mound : mountain

9. **tooth : fang**
   - (A) scale : snake
   - (B) bite : mouth
   - (C) quick : slow
   - (D) nail : claw

10. **zipper : pants**
    - (A) clock : hand
    - (B) button : shirt
    - (C) comb : teeth
    - (D) violin : bow

11. **customer : buyer**
    - (A) artist : easel
    - (B) dancer : planet
    - (C) swimmer : athlete
    - (D) store : mall

12. **immediate : later**
    - (A) cowardly : brave
    - (B) attempt : try
    - (C) respond : answer
    - (D) dull : boring

13. Make answer choices for this word pair: **Saturn : planet** . Make sure only one answer choice is correct.

    (A) _____ : _____   (C) _____ : _____

    (B) _____ : _____   (D) _____ : _____

14. Which answer is correct? _____ Why? _____

    _____

    _____

Answer Sheets

These sheets may be used to provide practice in answering questions in a standardized-test format.

Student's Name: _____

_____

Activity Page: _____

1. (A) (B) (C) (D)
2. (A) (B) (C) (D)
3. (A) (B) (C) (D)
4. (A) (B) (C) (D)
5. (A) (B) (C) (D)
6. (A) (B) (C) (D)
7. (A) (B) (C) (D)
8. (A) (B) (C) (D)
9. (A) (B) (C) (D)
10. (A) (B) (C) (D)
11. (A) (B) (C) (D)
12. (A) (B) (C) (D)

Student's Name: _____

_____

Activity Page: _____

1. (A) (B) (C) (D)
2. (A) (B) (C) (D)
3. (A) (B) (C) (D)
4. (A) (B) (C) (D)
5. (A) (B) (C) (D)
6. (A) (B) (C) (D)
7. (A) (B) (C) (D)
8. (A) (B) (C) (D)
9. (A) (B) (C) (D)
10. (A) (B) (C) (D)
11. (A) (B) (C) (D)
12. (A) (B) (C) (D)

Answer Key

Introducing Analogies (page 4)
1. calf
2. moo
3. hide, fur, leather, or milk
4. herd
5. bull
7. male
8. uncle
9. father
10. nephew
11. niece
12. Answers may vary (e.g., male : female)

Synonyms in Analogies (page 5)
1. D 5. B
2. C 6. A
3. A 7. B
4. D 8. C

Antonyms in Analogies (page 6)
1. A 5. D
2. B 6. C
3. C 7. D
4. A 8. B

Synonym and Antonym Practice (page 7)
1. D, antonym
2. A, synonym
3. B, synonym
4. C, antonym
5. A, synonym
6. A, antonym
7. B, antonym
8. D, synonym
9. C, synonym
10. C, antonym
11. D, antonym
12. B, synonym

Synonym and Antonym Analogies (page 8)
Accept appropriate responses.

Plurals (page 9)
1. B 7. C
2. A 8. D
3. B 9. A
4. A 10. B
5. D 11. D
6. C

Adjectives (page 10)
1. bright, adjective
2. ringed, adjective
3. D
4. A
5. C
6. A
7. B
8. D
9. C
10. D
11. A

What People Use (page 11)
1. D 6. B
2. B 7. C
3. A 8. A
4. C 9. C
5. D

Things that Go Together (page 12)
1. A 5. D
2. C 6. D
3. B 7. C
4. B 8. A

Past and Present (page 13)
1. brought
2. pushed
3. go
4. speak
5. pled
6. ride
7. leave
8. hurt
9. found
10. quit
11. present to past: 1, 2, 5, 9; past to present: 3, 4, 6, 7; can't tell: 8, 10; synonyms: 5

Past and Present 2 (page 14)
1. A 6. A
2. B 7. C
3. D 8. B
4. C 9. D
5. A 10. D

Purpose (page 15)
1. A 6. D
2. B 7. C
3. C 8. A
4. B 9. C
5. D 10. B

Where Things Go (page 16)
1. A 6. B
2. B 7. C
3. A 8. A
4. B 9. D
5. D 10. C

Animal Family Names (page 17)
1. A 6. C
2. B 7. D
3. B 8. B
4. C 9. A
5. A 10. D

Finding the Connection (page 18)
1. C
2. D
3. A
4. what covers or inside to outside
7. B
8. D
9. C
10. what goes in something
13. A
14. B
15. C
16. container and thing it contains

Finding the Connection 2 (page 19)
1. D
2. A
3. B
4. similar animal parts
6. C
7. A
8. D
9. animal to part, not part to animal
11. B
12. B
13. D
14. male to female

Answer Key *(cont.)*

Finding the Connection 3 (page 20)
1. A
2. B
3. C
4. place where people work
6. D
7. B
8. A
9. animals and their movements
11. D
12. C
13. D
14. things that stick together

Trying Out the Connection (page 21)
1. hill, mountain
2. employ, hire
3. triangle, shape
4. D
5. C
6. A

Part to Whole (page 22)
1. D
2. B
3. C
4. A
5. D
6. A
7. C
8. B
9. C
10. A
11. D
12. B
13. part to whole: 1, 3, 4, 6, 9, 12; whole to part: 2, 5, 7, 8, 10, 11
14. (order may vary) leaf : lettuce :: kernel : corn

Less Than/More Than (page 23)
1. B
2. A
3. B
4. D
5. A
6. D
7. D

8. C
9. A
10. A
11. D
12. (order may vary) say you will : swear to :: fond of : devoted to

Classifying Analogies (page 24)
1. birds
2. shoes
3. B
4. A
5. B
6. A
7. B
8. B
9. A
10. B
11. A
12. A

Classifying Analogies 2 (page 25)
1. tools
2. A screwdriver is always a tool; a tool is not always a screwdriver.
3. A
4. B
5. D
6. C
7. C
8. B
9. A
10. D
11. A

Practice Making Classes (page 26)
Accept appropriate responses.

Multiple-Meaning Words (page 27)
1. A
2. A
3. B
4. B
5. A
6. B
7. B
8. A
9. B
10. A

Multiple-Meaning Words 2 (page 28)
1. B
2. D, paint is a liquid
3. C, store has aisles
4. A, synonyms or, if store something, you save it
5. C, You smell smoke
6. B, synonyms
7. D, a point is a location
8. A, synonyms or, if you point, you aim
9. D, blow a whistle
10. A, whistle a tune
11. C, synonyms or when you guard, you watch
12. B, guard works in prison
13. animal; try to catch something

Math (page 29)
1. B
2. D
3. C
4. A
5. C
6. A
7. B
8. D

Math 2 (page 30)
1. C
2. A
3. D
4. B
5. D
6. B
7. C
8. D

Social Studies (page 31)
1. Albany
2. Austin
3. Sacramento
4. Denver
5. Tallahassee
6. Richmond
7. South Carolina
8. Oregon
9. Pennsylvania
10. Michigan
11. Frankfort
12. Indianapolis
13. North Dakota
14. Missouri
15. United States

Answer Key *(cont.)*

Social Studies 2 (page 32)
1. west
2. east
3. east
4. north
5. north
6. south
7. west
8. south
9. south
10. east
11. west
12. north

Science (page 33)
1. B
2. D
3. A
4. A
5. C
6. D
7. C
8. B

Science 2 (page 34)
1. C
2. A
3. D
4. D
5. D
6. A
7. B
8. C

Think and write: slightly more

Skeleton Analogies (page 35)
1. humerus
2. metatarsus
3. tibia
4. tarsus
5. head
6. scapula
7. pelvis
8. phalange

Challenge: adult person = 206, adult cat between 230–250 (depends on if it has a tail and how long the tail is)

Spelling (page 36)
1. B
2. D
3. C
4. A
5. C
6. A
7. D
8. B
9. C
10. A

Homophones (page 37)
1. principal
2. rein
3. their
4. reign
5. there
6. principle
7. they're
8. rain
9. principal

Challenge: write, hear

Homophones 2 (page 38)
1. fourth
2. bawl
3. lessen
4. ball
5. break
6. forth
7. brake
8. lesson
9. Let us now praise famous men.
10. I know you would like to eat this juicy steak.

Fun with Presidents (page 39)
1. Roosevelt (FDR) : Kennedy
2. Buchanan : Cleveland
3. William Henry Harrison : FDR
4. Garfield : Obama
5. John Quincy Adams : George Bush
6. Washington : Monroe
7. John Adams : Fillmore
8. Jackson : Carter

Challenge: Van Buren; others born before 1776, when the U.S. became a country

Fearful Analogies (page 40)
1. C
2. B
3. A
4. D
5. C
6. D
7. A
8. B
9. horse; river
10. water

Extreme Analogies (page 41)
1. C
2. D
3. B
4. D
5. A
6. B
7. C
8. A
9. C
10. D

Review of Analogy Types (page 42)
1. C, adjective
2. A, antonyms
3. D, past/present
4. B, synonyms
5. A, use
6. C, plural
7. B, synonyms
8. B, adjective
9. D, use
10. A, plural
11. C, antonyms
12. D, past/present
13. didn't know at first if it was past to present or present to past

Review of Analogy Types 2 (page 43)
1. D, member to group
2. B, less/more
3. A, homophone
4. C, where found
5. B, purpose
6. D, homophone
7. C, male/female
8. C, male/female
9. A, where found
10. B, less/more
11. D, member to group
12. A, purpose
13. yes

Use What You Know (page 44)
1. B, synonym; D, use brush to paint; A, B, D are not antonyms, so C is correct
2. C
3. question words are synonyms; B and D—antonyms; C—use glass to drink; answer must be A, as others not synonyms
4. B

Answer Key *(cont.)*

Use What You Know 2 (page 45)
1. doe is female deer; A, B, C—mother and child; answer must be D
2. C
3. kitten is baby cat; B, C, D—animal type to male; answer must be A
4. A
5. C
6. D
7. B
8. A

Use What You Know 3 (page 46)
1. wrong (all syn): A, B, D; correct (ant): C
2. wrong (all hom): A, C, D; correct (syn): B
3. wrong (all thing and what does): A, B, C; correct (member and group): D

Use What You Know 4 (page 47)
1. wrong (all male to female): A, C, D; correct (where person lives): B
2. D
3. B
4. A
5. C
6. month
7. noble
8. He was respected.
9. Yes. Accept reasonable responses.

Analogies in Writing (page 48)
3. A
4. B
5. B
6. A

Analogies in Reading (page 51)
1. B
2. B

Analogies in Reading 2 (page 52)
1. B

Analogies in Reading 3 (page 53)
1. C

Connection Review (page 54)
1. J
2. A
3. G
4. C
5. E
6. L
7. H
8. B
9. K
10. D
11. I
12. F

Connection Review 2 (page 55)
1. K
2. D
3. H
4. B
5. F
6. A
7. I
8. C
9. L
10. E
11. J
12. G

Practice Being the Teacher (page 56)
1. A: amuse, bore; B: chair, sit; C: rescue, save; D: dine, starve
2. A and D; antonyms
3. B; synonyms
4. D
5. A and B; present to past; past to present
6. C; heal, doctor

Practice Being the Teacher 2 (page 57)
1. A: broke, poor; B: cool, refrigerator; C: connect, join; D: sponge, wipe
2. A and C, synonyms
3. B
4. C
5. B
6. A and D

Practice What You Know (page 58)
1. C
2. D
3. B
4. A
5. D
6. A
7. B
8. C
9. C
10. A
11. B
12. D

Practice What You Know 2 (page 59)
1. D
2. A
3. C
4. B
5. A
6. B
7. C
8. D
9. D
10. B
11. C
12. A